ALA

PROGRAMMING GUIDES

ADULT PROGRAMS IN THE LIBRARY

WITHDRAWN FROM EVLD

BRETT W. LEAR

D1441674

AMERICAN LIBRARY ASSOCIATION

Chicago and London

2002

Brett W. Lear is a library manager with the Jefferson County Public Library (JCPL) in Colorado, where he served as chair of the Program Steering Committee (1998–2000). Lear has been actively involved in adult programming since accepting his first professional position with the New York Public Library in 1992. From 1995 through 1999, he served on the Reference and User Services Association's (RUSA) Services to Adults Committee, during which he participated in the writing of the RUSA publication *Adult Programming: A Manual for Libraries.* He currently serves as chair of RUSA's Library Services to the Spanish-Speaking Committee.

Cover by Tessing Design

Text design by Dianne M. Rooney

Composition by ALA Editions in Melior and Legacy Sans Medium using QuarkXpress 4.1 for the PC

Printed on 50-pound white offset, a pH-neutral stock, and bound in 10-point cover stock by Data Reproductions

The paper used in this publication meets the minimum requirements of American National Standard for Information Sciences—Permanence of Paper for Printed Library Materials, ANSI Z39.48-1992. ∞

Library of Congress Cataloging-in-Publication Data

Lear, Brett W.
    Adult programs in the library / Brett W. Lear
       p. cm. — (ALA programming guides)
    Includes bibliographical references and index.
    ISBN 0-8389-0810-1
    1. Public libraries—Services to adults—United States. 2.Libraries—Cultural programs—United States. 3. Libraries and community—United States.   I. Title.   II. Series.

    Z711.92.A32 L43 2001
    027.6′2—dc21   2001041269

Printed in the United States of America

06   05   04   03   02   5   4   3   2   1

For Grandpa

CONTENTS

PART 2
A Collection of Five-Star Programs 104

FIGURES

PREFACE

WHY SHOULD YOU READ THIS BOOK? THAT'S A question I would ask myself. How much can there be to know about library programming? If you want to have a program on, say, potty training, you just call a local day-care center and ask someone to come in and give a talk. Big deal. And, to some extent, that's true. But after you've organized programming for a few years, you begin to encounter some bumps in the road. Suppose this day-care provider:

Recommends corporal punishment as the best way to potty train a baby. You didn't know *that* was what she was going to talk about.

Begins selling potties for $19.95 at the end of the program.

Arrives twenty minutes late but wraps up ten minutes early and promptly requests the $100 check.

Asks afterward, "Well, how'd it go?" and you're wondering, too, because you hadn't thought of asking your patrons to evaluate the program.

Asks you how you publicized the event, because only one person was in the audience—you.

These things or close variations thereof can and will happen.

I wrote this book thinking that those who need a "How in the world do I . . . "–type answer can find it here. This book is for those of you who are just getting started with adult programming. Some of you will need to get your administrators on board. I also wrote for those who are well along in offering programming and now need help with grant writing and working with library foundation boards. And, I wrote to share ideas. There are some great ideas here, gathered from libraries around the United States.

This book addresses the specifics of programming for adults of all ages and interests. Because the book focuses exclusively on library programming for adult audiences, the sample programs are geared toward these audiences. Much of the information, however, can be applied to programming for any age group.

My experience with library programming has been that most libraries do some form of programming for children. I can't think of a library that doesn't do storytimes for children. Most libraries offer crafts programs for children. Many offer a summer reading club. However, this same level of basic programming is not as prevalent for adult audiences. Libraries that have offered children's programs for years might not offer *any* programs for adults (or young adults). These libraries may have limited funds, limited staff, or limited space. Or they may feel confident that programming for adults does not fit within their mission statement. If your library has offered children's programming for years, but is just beginning to offer programming for adults, you might find that your administrators need a little convincing that this is a service that should be integrated into basic library operations. It is also likely that your budget has not increased, and you may have to pursue alternate forms of funding. This book addresses these issues.

One of my primary goals when I began this project was to write something that was readable. The greatest compliment I can hope to receive from someone who has read this book is that he or she read it from front to back—by choice. I remember reading articles and chapters from books in library school and it was tough going. I remember reading ten-page articles in shifts. I hope this reads a bit easier. Library programming can be a lot of fun, and I hope I've conveyed this in these pages.

I know that some of you are asking "Why *should* our library offer programs?" This is the first question that any librarian new to programming asks. The sections on tying programs into your library's mission and conducting demographic studies will help you answer this question from an administrative point of view.

Programming can bring first-time patrons into your library. Programs can promote local talent as well as bring gifted individuals to your library from other cities and states. And, programs can be the best way to present a topic. A literacy workshop, for example, is probably more effective than a book when teaching literacy skills to a new reader. This book will help you find your focus by aligning your programs with your mission statement.

In part 2 of this book I've included examples of programs that strive to achieve various goals. These are real-life, successful programs conducted by today's librarians. I've also included an annotated Resource Directory that lists titles that can further assist you in such areas as budgeting and publicity. You'll also find many, many examples of the documents you will need—contracts, program policies, evaluation forms, checklists—to conduct successful programs.

I should mention here that I have not addressed patron instruction in this book at all. By *patron instruction* I mean library-produced classes that teach patrons how to use library resources, such as the Internet, genealogy materials, and so forth. These classes are, of course, invaluable to our patrons. I did not include patron instruction in this book because of the amount of training that is involved in preparing library staff for this type of service. Libraries that offer patron instruction frequently send staff members to Train-the-Trainer workshops where they learn patron-instruction techniques that they can then teach to other staff members. This is an elaborate process that I believe should be covered in work that addresses patron instruction. Because I have written a book that encourages you to bring in a wide variety of performers from throughout the community, I anticipate that many of these performers will not be staff members. I leave it to another author to describe ways in which you can prepare library staff to be instructors and performers for your patrons. (*Teaching the New Library: A How-to-Do-It Manual for Planning and Designing Instructional Programs* offers much information on patron instruction, including a chapter on training staff to become library teachers.[1] *Planning Programs for Adult Learners* is another good resource for people who are planning classes for adults.[2])

If I have done my part successfully, this book will show you how to develop an infrastructure that will allow your library to consistently conduct successful adult programs. Once this infrastructure is in place, you will find that programming is a rewarding, creative process that brings experiences and knowledge to your patrons that they otherwise wouldn't encounter in your library or perhaps even in your community.

I wish you success.

P.S. As I wrote this book, I noticed that many of the resources I consulted are no longer in print. I imagine this is because few books that cover library services make the *New York Times* bestsellers list. Unless these books are updated and republished in a revised edition, they tend to go out of print. Therefore, several of the titles I cite in the *Adult Programs in Libraries* are no longer in print. However, libraries throughout the United States do have these titles in their collections and were kind enough to allow me to borrow many via interlibrary loan. Although some of these titles may be out of print, they still do exist. I promise you that I looked through a copy of each of the books cited in the Resource Directory.

Endnotes

1. Cheryl LaGuardia and others, *Teaching the New Library: A How-to-Do-It Manual for Planning and Designing Instructional Programs* (New York: Neal-Schuman, 1996).

2. Caffarella, Rosemary S., *Planning Programs for Adult Learners: A Practical Guide for Educators, Trainers, and Staff Developers* (San Francisco: Jossey-Bass, 1994).

ACKNOWLEDGMENTS

FIRST, I WANT TO THANK ALL THE PEOPLE WHO responded when I put out pleas for help on various electronic mailing lists. The help they provided me is immeasurable. Some of these people are: Susan Akers, Anderson (Ind.) Public Library; Ann Hokanson, Prescott (Wis.) Public Library; Hillary Theyer, Torrance (Calif.) Public Library; Cecilia Wiltzius, Appleton (Wis.) Public Library; Carol Ann Robb, Pittsburg (Kans.) Public Library; Susan Emmons-Kroeger, Lisle (Ill.) Library District; Janet Bergeron, Oldsmar (Fla.) Public Library; Pat Allen, Sanibel (Fla.) Public Library; Michael Lambert, Foster City (Calif.) Library; Kathleen de la Peña McCook, University of South Florida; Janette Johnston, Round Rock (Tex.) Public Library; Carolyn Karwoski, The Ferguson Library (Conn.); Jamie Elston, Jefferson Parish (La.) Library; Carrie Farrow, Rochester (Minn.) Public Library; Robin D. Wood, San Marcos (Tex.) Public Library; and Chris Nowak, Rocky River (Ohio) Public Library.

Thanks must go to my employer, the Jefferson County Public Library, for providing me with the equipment necessary to complete this project. I also want to thank all the staff members who answered questions and provided me with many of the documents that are used as examples in this book. I particularly want to thank Margaret Owens, Paddy Correia, and Kay Pride. But, most of all, I want to thank the staff of the Lakewood Library for hanging in there with me as I became more and more harried and less coherent down the home stretch.

I want to thank Marlene Chamberlain of ALA Editions for offering me this wonderful opportunity.

And thank you, Robyn, for being there—in person, on the phone, and via e-mail.

INTRODUCTION

Who Invented the Program?

A good place to start a book on programming is at the beginning. That seems to be where most books begin. I like books. I like the fact that they can be both entirely predictable and utterly mysterious—simultaneously. Nonfiction books are terrific at pulling this off. When I open one, I know that I'm going to hear some history behind the topic. I know that the book will help me understand how the topic is relevant to our time period, and, perhaps, to me. I know there'll be some introduction that tells me what I'm about to experience and some summation that will review what I should have learned. The wrap-ups are great, because they either make me feel smart because I *did* get what I was supposed to get, or they help me cheat by teaching me in a paragraph what I didn't get in the previous four hundred pages. And the mystery lies in the learning. Learning what I didn't know. Not knowing what the next page will bring. Anticipating the unknown.

When beginning this book, I knew that I should do the predictable bit: write a section on the early history of library programming. When I sat down to do that, I quickly realized that this would be an unknown subject to me. I would need to read and learn. And I wasn't necessarily anticipating this endeavor. But I began to explore. I searched print indexes and electronic databases, and I wasn't finding much. I was beginning to feel bogged down. Would I spend the first few weeks looking for enough information to eke out a paragraph on the inception of library programming? Then I found it. The nonfiction book. The book was titled *Public Libraries as Culture and Social Centers: The Origin of the Concept* by D. W. Davies. I opened it, and that wonderful mix of predictability and mystery began. Here's what I learned.

The first examples of library programming in the United States and England began appearing in the late 1800s. It appears that the times were not entirely different from our own. Back in the 1890s, the average library patron seemed to favor fiction over nonfiction. Some librarians of the day thought this was because the public needed a bit more guidance. A form of reader's advisory was born. Librarians would ask patrons to stop reading and listen to their lectures on what to read and on the use and abuse of fiction. The lecture series was born! Librarians thankfully moved on from captive-audience lectures to exhibits and displays. The librarian Charles A. Cutter believed that exhibits bring people to the library who might not otherwise attend. Photography was still a relatively new medium in 1900 in America, and Charles was certain that photography displays would attract people to the library. By the early 1900s, librarians had also learned that they could tie a display to the books in the library. For example, Native American rugs could be placed on display along with a table full of books about Native Americans.[1]

In 1840s Britain, legislation was passed that allowed for taxes to be raised for the support of public libraries and museums. Frequently, the support for libraries and museums came from the same tax. Since both entities were often under one authority, it became common for a museum to have a library in an adjacent room of the same building. The libraries had easy access to art to put on display. And they had access to the societies that supported the museums. Many of these societies offered art classes, so it was a natural extension that the libraries would invite the societies into the library to teach these classes. Tax-supported libraries often were given the buildings or private library collections of societies. The societies would then offer classes or lectures in the library. Britain's Libraries Amendment Act of 1884 allowed libraries to apply for national grants to support classes in drawing, painting, architectural design, and other areas of technology and design. Libraries in the United States, although not supported by government funding, soon realized that Americans had an equal hunger for knowledge and instruction. Classes in art, child rearing, and many other subjects soon appeared in the United States as well.[2]

It turns out that the idea of the library as a social or entertainment center is not new either. By the early 1800s, societies were offering balls and concerts with the intent of enlightening people about the wonders of art. Social settlements sprang up during this period, offering workshops in the arts and sciences to the working poor. Clubs, such as men's clubs, appeared in the latter part of the nineteenth century and offered concerts, lectures, and such games as billiards. As American and English libraries came of age during this time, many of them began offering games, lectures, visits to poor neighborhoods, and festivals for ethnic groups.[3]

What Is Programming?

Davies' book helps us trace the inception of library programming back to the nineteenth century. Many of the types of programs (lectures, workshops, and concerts) we host in our libraries today were being held in libraries over a hundred years ago in the United States and England. After looking into the past, let's look at the present. What types of programs are being produced in libraries today? Why do libraries sponsor programs? Perhaps we should first attempt to define what we mean by *programming.*

When I began writing this book I realized that I would have to change my life. For the next year

I knew that I'd be very, very busy. I'd say to people, "I'm writing this book on adult programming and I'm going to have to really knuckle down. . . ." Fellow library staff members had a pretty good idea of what I was up to. But my friends outside the library didn't really get what I was writing *about.* Adult programming? Perhaps they thought I was writing about programmers of adult software. Sometimes I'd say I was writing a book on adult programs. I received the same blank stare. Perhaps they thought I was creating a book on how to create a newsletter for adults—sort of like the program they sell you at the racetrack, but different. Their confusion led to my confusion. What is a *library program?* The term itself isn't very attractive. It doesn't grab your attention. If you walked up to someone who'd never been in a library before and said, "Hey, guess what? The library down the street is really big into library programs," what would the response be? I suspect the individual would offer a quizzical look and say something like, "Hmm. Really." Why don't we call library programs *library events,* or *library classes,* or *library spectaculars?* We do use some of these terms. The word *program* encompasses lectures, classes, panel discussions, workshops, and more. But what does it *mean?*

"If You Don't Know the Answer, Look It Up"

I checked my 1965 edition of *Webster's Seventh New Collegiate Dictionary.* It said that the word *program* means a public notice. That seemed relevant. When I organize a program, part of the process involves giving public notice, generating publicity. The dictionary also said that a program is a "brief outline of the order to be pursued or the subjects embraced."[4] That's part of programming, too. I ask performers to submit an outline to me of their program, specifying what topics they will cover. This outline is brought before our program committee, and, if the concept is approved, the outline helps our public information (public relations) office in generating publicity. The dictionary then told me that a program is "the performance of a program." It also defines a program as a plan or procedure. This reminded me of our programming policy and the various internal documents that have been written over the years to address such things as authors selling their books after a program, the use of live animals in programs, and the preparation and eating of food during programs. A program is, according to Webster's, a proposed project or scheme. This must be the planning part of programming. Someone on staff gets an idea for a program and becomes the program's coordinator, working out the details of who will perform the program, what topics will be covered, which branches will offer the program, and so forth. Webster says a program is a comprehensive schedule, and that's also true. Our program committee spends a great deal of time with scheduling. We try to tie programs into monthly celebrations, such as Cinco de Mayo. We try to book only a certain number of programs each month, to ensure that each program will get adequate coverage in our newsletter and the local newspapers. We track who has booked our meeting rooms and when. The dictionary also defines *program* as a "printed bill, card, or booklet giving a program." That sounds like our newsletter.

After spending time with my dictionary, I was curious to know if anyone had managed to compress all these aspects of programming into a one-sentence definition. I located a concise document entitled *Rated "A" for Adult: A Guide to Library Programming* by Chris Painter and Maureen Crocker. The authors manage to partially define programming in a paragraph:

> Programming is an activity most public libraries do, but it is very broadly defined. Typically, even the smallest library provided programs for children such as weekly story hours, or summer reading programming. For all practical purposes, "programming" here refers to a specific recreational, educational, or cultural group event or activity sponsored by the library, and is geared toward the adult audience. Programs may be ongoing, a series, or a one-time event.[5]

The preceding paragraph defines programming in terms of the type of program, the format, and the age level. It doesn't include insight into the planning, publicity, staffing, and scheduling involved. But library programming is also more

than the sum of its parts. Programming can be a central ingredient of your library's mission. In 1979, the Public Library Association (PLA) produced *The Public Library Mission Statement and Its Imperatives for Service. Information* is defined as "not only the sum total of recorded human experiences—factual, imaginative, scientific, and humanistic—but also the unrecorded experience which is available only from human resources to which library users may be referred."[6] This definition places people and books on equal footing as information resources. Programming can become an extension of your library's collection and resources. Through programming, you can fulfill your mission of meeting the informational, educational, and recreational needs of your patrons. By combining PLA's definition of *information* with a typical mission statement, we can create a good definition of programming:

> Programming is a process by which the informational, educational, and recreational needs of patrons are met by bringing patrons into contact with the human resources best able to meet those needs.

It's a bit long-winded, but it establishes programming as an essential library service that fits snugly within your library's mission.

The complexity of the definition of *program* and *programming* seems appropriate. Library programming is a complex undertaking. Before the first program ever occurs in your library, you need to conduct demographic studies, write policies, form committees, create forms, make media contacts, establish funding sources, and establish methods of evaluating success. Then, after the live turtle falls off a table and cracks his shell or a financial investor begins selling stocks during a lecture, you will sit down and write more policies. Programming, like any major initiative, takes planning. The chapters in this book are designed to help you plan.

To Program or Not to Program?

If programming is so complicated, why do it? This is a good question. Many libraries justifiably feel that it's all they can do to keep their information desks adequately staffed while ordering and maintaining the materials in their collection. The direct cost of a program can be very minimal. It's fairly easy to find a knowledgeable speaker who will appear at your library free of charge. Universities, for example, usually have lists of faculty members who will speak at your organization without charge. The staff member planning the program can usually coordinate the program and negotiate the arrangements with the performer in a short amount of time. For example, I've gotten an idea for a program, located a performer, and selected dates and locations—all in less than two hours. It would seem as if the program's total cost (if the performer does not charge a fee) would be the two hours I invested in planning the program.

Actually, in addition to such costs as performers' fees and staff time, you will also have publicity fees for flyers, newsletters, and whatever paid advertising you choose to run. And, if you work in a multibranch system, the following staff members may be involved in the production of your program:

  A staff member—probably you—begins coordinating the program by contacting the performer and submitting the forms needed for publicity, meeting rooms, and extra equipment (chairs, audiovisual equipment, etc.).

  A program committee may exist to approve the idea, performer, and cost, and see that the program is consistent with the library's mission.

  Other staff in other branches may be notified of the program to see if they would like the program in their branches as well.

  Meeting rooms may have to be booked in various branches. Some libraries will have an administrative assistant who organizes the meeting room reservations from a central location.

  Someone in administration drafts and mails a contract to the performer.

  The people in your public relations office write news releases and distribute them to the local media. They also write the text for the newsletter and flyers.

  Your graphics staff create the flyers and include the program description in the library newsletter.

  Your public relations staff mail some of these flyers and newsletters to organizations and individuals in the community.

  Some of your building services staff may need to bring extra chairs and equipment to your meeting room and help you set them up.

  As the program approaches, the coordinating staff member confirms with the performer, pulls together materials (related books, videos, bibliographies, etc.) to display during the program, introduces the speaker, watches the program and writes an evaluation, compiles the patrons' evaluations, and, later, writes a thank-you note to the speaker.

  Building services staff remove the equipment and chairs.

The indirect costs—primarily staff time—of a program can be significant. Most libraries that consistently offer a variety of adult programs have a process similar to the preceding one in place. Newsletters and flyers and contracts and audiovisual equipment are standard components of library programming. We all want to produce high-quality, well-attended programs. But do you have the resources necessary to pull it off? Should you offer adult programs at your library?

The answer is yes, if (1) you've worked programming into your library's mission and (2) you've either confirmed that you have the staff and other resources necessary to complete the tasks listed above, or you've found ways to eliminate many of these tasks and still produce quality programs that draw an audience. If both of these statements are true, then you are ready to proceed. Here are some reasons to say yes to library programming:

  Programs can promote your collection. Have a performer give a talk on the Holocaust and create a display of books and videos to accentuate the performance.

  Programs can be the best way to present certain types of information. For example, a presentation on the ten best business-related Internet sites ensures that the information is current. Or, hearing and seeing a live musical performance can be much more meaningful than listening to a CD.

- Programs can get people into your library who might not otherwise visit. Free classes on English as a Second Language would be a good way to attract some of your non-English-speaking community members into the library.

- If your library is in a community that doesn't have much access to the theater or to nationally known authors or orchestras, the library may be the perfect community center to host these artists and events.

- Programs are ideal for those who can't afford or choose not to pay for certain types of information. Just as someone may choose to use your library instead of buying a book at a bookstore, so will some people choose to attend a program on selecting a home computer instead of paying for a similar workshop at a community college.

- Programming can also establish goodwill between your library and other local agencies. For example, many agencies have information to share with the community, but they don't have the facilities. You can invite these groups into your library and publicize their lecture or workshop as a library program.

- Programming increases your library's visibility in the community, through the news releases, flyers, and the positive word of mouth of satisfied patrons.

- And, like most things, programming gets easier the more you do it. The process becomes streamlined and second nature, performers start coming to you asking for permission to perform, patrons get excited and begin offering suggestions, and the staff can directly see the benefits of their time and effort.

As we can see from the preceding list, adult programming benefits your patrons and your library. Although it may at first appear that your library doesn't offer adult programs, look a bit closer. There is a very good chance that your library is already doing some type of adult programming. In 1999, the American Library Association (ALA) published *Cultural Programs for Adults in Public Libraries.* When the Public Programs Office of ALA conducted a survey of libraries serving populations of 5,000 and more, 1,229 usable responses were received. Cultural programs were defined as programs that fit within these categories: book discussions, creative writing programs, author presentations/readings, reading incentive programs, lecture series, musical performances, dance performances, dramatic performances, and film series. These types of programs encompass many of the topics that come to mind when we think of adult programs. Therefore, it isn't surprising that the surveyed libraries offered a wide range of programs—poetry readings, arts and crafts programs, genealogy workshops, travelogues. What might be surprising is the number of libraries offering cultural programming. Nine out of ten libraries (85.6 percent) reported offering some type of cultural programming for adults.[7]

Perhaps your library is the one out of ten that is not currently offering adult programs, but you intend to change that. Some of you will read this (or parts of this) book because you are just beginning to offer programming in your library or organization. Ideally—although it means tons of work for you—your library director just walked up to your desk and dropped this book in front of you and said, "Here. Let's do some of this adult programming stuff. Have at it and have fun." Now you need to gather some information on how to best begin the process of offering adult programs. I hope this book will help you.

Getting Administration on Board

You may, however, be at the other end of the spectrum. Your director or administration or both may not be outright opposed to the idea of adult programming, but they just aren't nearly as enthusiastic as you are at the prospect of bringing in someone to do some artsy thing for ninety minutes at $60 an hour. Although most libraries offer some type of adult programs, many of these libraries do not see programming as central to their mission. Approximately half of the libraries that offer adult programming feel it is central to their mission; the other half say it isn't.[8]

If your glass is half empty, there are techniques you can use to fill it. Administrators are managers, and managers are usually convinced to go in new directions through proposals and studies. If you are in a position of some influence, such as a library manager, perhaps you can present this proposal to a director or a coordinator of adult services. If you work for a system that is largely decentralized, perhaps you only need to get your branch manager on board. If you don't have a good feel for your library's hierarchy and culture, work with your supervisor or your mentor or a knowledgeable peer and learn how things get done in your library system. Eventually, programming will get a yes.

We librarians are a creative bunch, so I know you have plenty of ideas. And you have the go-ahead to make these ideas *happen*. But—you guessed it—I'm going to advise you to take a breath and read on before you call the local raptor society to give a talk on the American bald eagle—because the raptor man, it turns out, wants to bring three young birds with him, and he suggests that the audience have an opportu-nity to purchase the bird-watching book he just published, and his fee is negotiable, he says, while reminding you that people love his program because, in part, it's *dangerous*. Gulp. Please read on, and we'll establish the guidelines and get the insurance necessary to make even this program a reality.

Endnotes

1. D. W. Davies, *Public Libraries as Culture and Social Centers: The Origin of the Concept* (Metuchen, N.J.: Scarecrow, 1974), 64–65.

2. Ibid., 64, 76–77.

3. Ibid., 97, 100, 104–5.

4. *Webster's Seventh New Collegiate Dictionary* (Springfield, Mass.: Merriam, 1965), 680.

5. Chris Painter and Maureen Crocker, *Rated "A" for Adult: A Guide to Library Programming* (Pinecliff, Colo.: Colorado Library Association, 1991), 9.

6. *The Public Library Mission Statement and Its Imperatives for Service* (Chicago: American Library Association, 1979), 5.

7. Debra Wilcox Johnson, *Cultural Programs for Adults in Public Libraries: A Survey Report* (Chicago: American Library Association, Public Programs Office, [1999]), iv.

8. Ibid., v.

1

Tying Programming to Your Library's Mission

WHEN AN INSTITUTION FIRST BEGINS TO CONSIDER offering adult programs, the following questions will arise, in one form or another: What are we trying to do here? Will programs be offered as a way to get people into the building? Will they closely reflect the library's collection? Will they be used to fill a cultural or informational gap in the community? A programming policy can help answer these questions.

Writing a programming policy is a good idea. This policy can be integrated into your collection development policy. Frequently, the first sentence of your programming policy and the first sentence of your mission statement will be nearly identical. For example, the mission statement of the Oshawa Public Library in Oshawa, Ontario, begins: "The Oshawa Public Library seeks to deliver a high level of service in a cost-effective manner by providing facilities, materials, and knowledgeable responsive staff assistance directed at meeting the informational, educational, recreational, and cultural needs of the citizens of our community." This is very similar to the opening sentence of Merrimack Public Library's programming policy: "The Merrimack Public Library will present programs that offer information, education, and recreation to the citizens of Merrimack."

Both the mission statement and the programming policy quoted above contain the word *recreational.* Your mission statement and your programming policy are your guides. Be sure they say what you want and intend to do. If you include the word *recreational* in your policy, then the types of programs you can offer become very broad indeed. Libraries with such broad policies can offer such programs as singles mixers. This might consist of the library advertising that once a month, on Fridays, from 5:00 to 7:00 P.M., the main branch will host a singles mixer consisting of music, dancing, and light refreshments. Such a function would probably be well attended, and it might bring people into the library for the first time. This program doesn't necessarily fulfill a cultural or informational need, but it is fun. If your library would be reluctant to offer purely recreational programming, then you might want to omit this word from your mission statement and programming policy, or you might want to add a sentence defining what you mean by *recreational.*

Some mission statements affirm that the library provides informational and cultural materials and services. The programming policy can then be written to state that the library provides

1

informational and cultural programs. You may also want to mention in your programming policy that the programs offered are consistent with materials that your library collects. This gives your library quite a bit of flexibility, even if the word *recreational* is not included in the policy. Think of a programming topic. Now go to your library's catalog and do a search on that topic. You will probably have to be really creative to think of a programming topic that is not addressed in a book in your print collection. Somewhere in your collection, you will likely have a book that explains how to start a singles club. And, you most likely have a community resource directory that lists singles clubs. If you decide to pursue programming that is informational and cultural—but not recreational—in content, then your library might choose to offer a program on how to start a singles club or how to locate singles clubs in your community. But, hosting a singles dance party will probably not fit within your mission.

Now that you've decided on the type (recreational, informational, cultural, etc.) of programming you will offer, you are ready to get into the finer details. Here are some other questions you might want to address in your policy:

Will you produce programs on topics that are already covered by other agencies? For example, will you ask a local doctor to present a lecture on high blood pressure, or will you invite the American Heart Association into your library to present a program on that topic?

Will you charge an admission fee to your programs? Will you charge a materials fee at some of your programs? For example, if you get someone to offer a workshop on calligraphy and each patron needs paper and pens for the workshop, will your library purchase the materials, and will you then pass this expense on to the patron?

Who selects the performers—a centralized committee? individuals in the branches? the library director? your Friends group?

Can for-profit groups and individuals present programs or will you limit performers to those people who are members of non-profit organizations and associations? If you permit for-profit groups, can these groups promote their products or services during the program? Can they at least mention their products and services and offer their business cards to patrons?

Can performers during or after the program sell products? If not, do you want to make an exception for authors selling their books?

How will you attempt to ensure that the content of the programs is accurate? Will you evaluate the performer's handout before the program? Will you ask for and check references? Will you interview other agencies that have hosted the performer?

Figure 1.1 shows a programming policy that addresses some of the questions and issues raised here.

FIGURE 1.1
Sample Programming Policy

All programs being considered for Jefferson County Public Library should meet the following criteria to ensure quality:

Offers information best transmitted in groups.

Promotes appreciation of books and reading.

Introduces a range of library services.

Enhances the use of the library's collection.

Improves access to information for targeted audiences.

Encourages positive community cooperation and support.

In addition to the above criteria, we will consider attendance, appropriateness of subject to the audience, circulation in subject area of the program, and comments from the public and library staff in determining whether or not the program was worthwhile.

Branch representatives to the Programming Committee should discuss with their own Branch Manager parameters for program planning within the branch and consult the Branch Program Goals. These goals might include space and time constraints, impact on other library services including Graphics, and special interests of the branch.

Source: Jefferson County (Colo.) Public Library

Your programming policy will be the compass that keeps you on the right path. Be sure that it points in the right direction. If you want to offer programs that will supplement or enhance your library's collection, say this in your policy. Sometimes, the best way to convey information is through human interaction. For example, the best way to convey information on learning English might be through literacy classes and ESL (English as a Second Language) classes. If your library intends to offer such programs, don't say in your policy that your programs will be limited to topics that are represented in your materials collection. Other topics for programs might include a class on how to use your library's Web page or a workshop instructing people on how to

fill out their census form. These topics are not going to be covered in books in the library. If you want to offer these programs, state in your policy that one of the reasons you offer programming is to provide information that is best transmitted by human interaction.

The American Library Association created a document called "Library-Initiated Programs as a Resource: An Interpretation of the *Library Bill of Rights.*"[1] This document fits library programming within the context of the *Library Bill of Rights.*[2] It is also a good model to look at when drafting a programming policy. This document is available at www.ala.org/alaorg/oif/lib_res.html and is included in figure 1.2.

FIGURE 1.2
Library-Initiated Programs as a Resource: An Interpretation of the *Library Bill of Rights*

Library-initiated programs support the mission of the library by providing users with additional opportunities for information, education and recreation. Article I of the *Library Bill of Rights* states: "Books and other library resources should be provided for the interest, information and enlightenment of all people of the community the library serves."

Library-initiated programs take advantage of library staff expertise, collections, services and facilities to increase access to information and information resources. Library-initiated programs introduce users and potential users to the resources of the library and to the library's primary function as a facilitator of information access. The library may participate in cooperative or joint programs with other agencies, organizations, institutions or individuals as part of its own effort to address information needs and to facilitate information access in the community the library serves.

Library-initiated programs on site and in other locations include, but are not limited to, speeches, community forums, discussion groups, demonstrations, displays, and live or media presentations.

Libraries serving multilingual or multicultural communities make efforts to accommodate the information needs of those for whom English is a second language. Library-initiated programs across language and cultural barriers introduce otherwise unserved populations to the resources of the library and provide access to information.

Library-initiated programs "should not be proscribed or removed (or canceled) because of partisan or doctrinal disapproval" of the contents of the program or the views expressed by the participants, as stated in Article 2 of the *Library Bill of Rights*. Library sponsorship of a program does not constitute an endorsement of the content of the program or the views expressed by the participants, any more than the purchase of

material for the library collection constitutes an endorsement of the contents of the material or the views of its creator.

Library-initiated programs are a library resource, and as such, are developed in accordance with written guidelines, as approved and adopted by the library's policy-making body. These guidelines include an endorsement of the *Library Bill of Rights* and set forth the library's commitment to free and open access to information and ideas for all users.

Library staff select topics, speakers and resource materials for library-initiated programs based on the interests and information needs of the community. Topics, speakers and resource materials are not excluded from library-initiated programs because of possible controversy. Concerns, questions or complaints about library-initiated programs are handled according to the same written policy and procedures which govern reconsiderations of other library resources.

Library-initiated programs are offered free of charge and are open to all. Article V of the *Library Bill of Rights* states: "A person's right to use a library should not be denied or abridged because of origin, age, background, or views."

The "right to use a library" encompasses all of the resources the library offers, including the right to attend library-initiated programs. Libraries do not deny or abridge access to library resources, including library-initiated programs, based on an individual's economic background and ability to pay.

Adopted January 27, 1982. Amended June 26, 1990, by the ALA Council.

Source: American Library Association, "Library-Initiated Programs as a Resource: An Interpretation of the *Library Bill of Rights*," in *Intellectual Freedom Manual*, 6th ed. (Chicago: American Library Association, 2002), http://www.ala.org/alaorg/oif/lib_res.html.

This may be obvious, but once you have drafted a programming policy, you will want to have this document flow through whatever process is necessary in order for it to become an official document within your organization. You will want this document to be as official as your mission statement and collection development policy. Your programming policy should stand alongside your library's other bedrock documents. This may mean that the director or even the library board will need to sign off on this policy. If you are the director, you are well on your way. If you are, say, a member of a subcommittee that is drafting this document as an initial step in offering adult programming, be sure to use your supervisor and peers to help you steer the policy through the proper channels.

It is sometimes a good idea to ask around and get an idea of what seems possible before you begin writing. Are you proposing a policy that the administration will find unrealistic and, therefore, impossible to implement? If possible, discuss the potential parameters of the policy with the people who will approve it. If this is not possible, then speak with those people who have a good feel for how your administration thinks.

Even if your administrators asked you to frame the policy, it doesn't hurt to ask them what they have in mind before you begin. Communication along the way can only help, and it increases your chances of getting your initial draft approved without major changes. This saves time, which means you will be that much closer to offering programs to your patrons. You can always propose to expand or alter the policy at a later time.

Once you have an approved programming policy in place, you have established *what* your programming focus will be. Now you are ready to begin drawing the sketch of *how* you will translate your policy into programming.

Endnotes

1. American Library Association, "Library-Initiated Programs as a Resource: An Interpretation of the *Library Bill of Rights*," in *Intellectual Freedom Manual,* 6th ed. (Chicago: American Library Association, 2002), http://www.ala.org/alaorg/oif/lib_res.html.

2. American Library Association, *Library Bill of Rights,* in *Intellectual Freedom Manual,* 6th ed. (Chicago: American Library Association, 2002), http://www.ala.org/work/freedom/lbr.html.

2

Developing Guidelines and Procedures

ALL RIGHT. YOU'VE WRITTEN A PROGRAMMING POLICY and now you're ready to go get your performer. Not so fast. Before you plan your program, you will want to have some procedures and documents in place first. As you begin to think of ideas and develop them, some "what ifs" will emerge. For example:

What if the author you scheduled wants to sell her book after the program?

What if the cook giving the "Healthy Eating during the Holidays" program wants to prepare a dish and feed it to the audience?

What if the representative from the zoo suggests bringing a twelve-foot python and a hawk to a children's nature program?

Figures 2.1 and 2.2 present policies for live animals and food that were developed by the Jefferson County (Colo.) Public Library.

You'll find that your written programming policies will expand over time. Getting these policies in writing will save staff time because staff will know from the start what is acceptable and not acceptable within your library. You will also be doing your performers a service, because you will be applying the same guidelines and policies to each of them. You won't say no to one author who wants to sell her books after a reading, and then say yes to another author six months later.

Before we go much farther with drafting various documents, let's pause and reach some consensus on why we are doing this. Let's not write these policies because we want to be able to tell

---

FIGURE 2.1

Sample Policy: Use of Animals in Library Programs

The Program Coordinator for a program that includes animals should contact the Associate Director for Administrative Services in advance, with a brief description of any event that may involve wildlife. Include the date(s) of the program, the location(s), the animal(s), and a description of the animal handler (i.e., "a certified trainer from the Rocky Mountain Raptor Society").

The Library's insurance covers all activities usually associated with a public library. The Associate Director for Administrative Services will work with the Library's insurance carrier to provide the insurance coverage the program requires. Whenever there is a question in the mind of our insurance underwriter about whether a program is within the usual scope of activities of a public library, the Associate Director can choose to authorize special coverage if necessary.

FIGURE 2.2

Sample Policy: Use of Food in the Library

Anything the Library may offer in regard to food is under guidelines established and enforced by the Jefferson County Health Department. Library programs fall under the Jefferson County Health Department's "occasional events" guidelines. We do not need to contact a health inspector to approve our use of food, as long as we adhere to the following guidelines:

1. Food to be served must be purchased from inspected, approved sources.

2. Everyone handling food must wash his/her hands.

3. If perishable food is distributed at the library, the food must be transported and stored properly (must remain hot, if necessary, or cold if necessary).

The Library does not serve food as refreshments at its programs. Water, coffee and tea may be prepared and offered at programs such as Book Discussion Groups, if staff is willing to prepare and clean up.

Food may be used in programs if it is integral to the subject of the program. Be sensitive to the possibility that food may create a mess and plan to protect carpeting and furniture. Library staff is responsible for cleaning up after programs. Practical examples include:

IT IS OKAY TO:

- distribute individually wrapped candy at Halloween.
- serve a cake from King Soopers (because King Soopers is an inspected, approved source).
- conduct food programs with children, such as churning butter, as long as the food is purchased from an approved source (grocery store as opposed to our personal garden or goat in the backyard), and that everyone washes his/her hands.

IT IS *NOT* OKAY TO:

- serve the public food that has been prepared in our own homes (since we are not inspected, approved sources).

staff and performers what they can or cannot do. It may seem as if that's the intent of these documents. It's not. A coworker I admire a great deal stresses the importance of keeping "the eyes on the prize." Policies should not become so cumbersome and difficult to fulfill that they impede your goal, which is to provide quality programs to your patrons in a manner that is consistent with the mission and priorities of your library. Good policies should be as simple as possible. Policies should exist to clarify actions and make goals easier to achieve. Believe it or not, staff and performers will quickly express negative com-

ments if they feel that the programming process is a disorganized mess. The policies and procedures you develop should pave your way to organized, successful programming.

Let's assume that you or your library or both are new to adult programming. You have a written programming policy in place, and you've written a few other policies that address issues that will come up right away, such as authors selling their books and performers preparing food. You are now getting closer to actually putting on a program. It's probably time to take a look at your financial resources.

Creating a Budget

If you have no money to dedicate to programming, yet you've still created your policies, this probably means that you are prepared to persevere and pursue programs that are free. Either you will have library staff present the programs or you will work with agencies and individuals who are willing to perform without a fee. These programs will still require staff time and facilities, as well as publicity costs. If you choose to pursue only free programs, you may want to include this in your policy. This will save both your staff and potential performers a good deal of time during the initial negotiations.

If you are fortunate enough to have funds to put toward programming, it is a good idea to create a budget line with a specific sum of money. Try to get a "programming" line added to your operating budget and place a specific dollar amount on this line at the beginning of the year. Once you have created a budget line, you'll have to decide how to divide the money among the types of programming: children's, adult, young adult (YA), and so on.

After you've placed money into a programming budget line, you'll need to decide how this money can be spent. Will this money only pay for performers' fees? What if you are hiring a local poet to give a poetry reading, and you'd like to purchase and serve cheese and crackers during the reading? How do you pay for these snacks? Perhaps the poet's appearance was planned to coincide with the conclusion of a poetry contest. You'd like the poet to announce the winners and hand out books of poems as prizes. Will the programming budget pay for the books? Some libraries just take the money from the cash register, ring it up to petty cash, and go purchase snacks or prizes. Other libraries might pay the performer from the programming budget, charge the books to a supply budget, and pay for the food from money awarded to the library from the library foundation. It's a good idea to establish a consistent procedure. Libraries that are publicly funded might want to be especially careful with their budgeting practices; will it look odd to a taxpayer or board member if "$200 for candy and soda" is charged to your supply budget?

For much more detailed information on budgeting and funding, please turn to chapter 5.

Forming a Committee

This is beginning to sound like a lot of work. And it is. This doesn't mean that it's drudgery—it's probable that you'll like, even love, the work you do with library programming. But it *is* work. You'll write policies, create budgets, contact performers, write contracts, create publicity, and evaluate performers. Unless you are the only staff person available to do this work, you'll probably want to share the workload. Even if you are one person in a one-library system, you can still use others to help you. If you have e-mail, you can communicate with teachers, museums, and others in your community, all at once. You can find out which performers they've hired recently and which programs were successes. You can then begin collaborating on cosponsoring events. This can also be done, albeit a little more slowly, over the telephone.

This is also the point at which you will probably want to decide just *how* you will do your programming. If yours is a single-building library system, you will book programs for this single branch. But, if you are in a multiple-branch system, you can go about your programming in at least two very different ways. First, you can seek out performers and book them at a branch level without collaborating with the other branches in the system. You will still probably submit requests and other paperwork to a central office,

but you will be submitting a request for only your branch. The second approach is to work collaboratively with other branches when booking programs. Following this model, after you have identified a topic and located a performer, you would contact other branches to see if they would like to host the program as well. The first model definitely gives you plenty of freedom. The second model, however, spreads the work throughout the system and offers patrons some choices as to where they can attend the program.

Regardless of which model you choose, you have some work ahead of you. If you have others who can share the workload, and if you are going to be working with other departments, such as the accounting office or the public relations office, you might want to form a programming committee. Although a committee can seem like an additional layer of bureaucracy, in reality it can save you time and generate some creative ideas. Who would be on this committee and what would they do? Let me answer this by describing an hour in the life of a hypothetical committee in a typical public library. (Let's assume that this committee exists within a library system that collaborates among branches when booking programs.)

A Programming Committee Meeting

Your meeting begins at 9:00 A.M. on a Thursday. You work for a ten-branch public library system. You begin the meeting by discussing the programming that is occurring in the library this month. It's an average month. Eighty storytimes for children are scheduled. This month the library has also scheduled two series of family programs and one adult series. A "series" is defined as a program that occurs at more than one library location. The two family series are a wildlife watching series, where kids can learn tips on how to spot such wildlife as birds and rabbits, and a series with Doc Susie. Doc Susie is a performance artist who dresses up as a pioneering doctor and tells stories of her life. The wildlife program will be held in five branches and the Doc Susie program will be held in three branches. You expect both programs to attract people of all ages. For adults you have a series of programs on flowers: One program will cover growing roses, another will cover identifying wildflowers, and a third will cover the history of the rose as a decorative flower. Seven branches have chosen to hold one of the three programs in the roses series. In addition to all this activity, your library system will host a series of AARP (American Association of Retired Persons) tax assistance sessions in seven of your branches. *And,* thirty-five patron education classes—for both adults and children—are scheduled throughout the library, ranging from classes on how to use the online catalog to a basic Internet instruction class for parents and their kids.

Before we proceed with the meeting, let's pause and take a look at the members of this committee. Of the five members, one person is a head of reference and adult services at one of the branches, one person is a head of children's services, and a third member is a specialist in young adult services. The fourth member is a representative from the public information office. This is the office that generates the publicity for your library. Some libraries call this office the public relations or communications office. This office may also be the "voice" of your library, making statements to the local press and paying visits to local businesses and organizations to improve your library's visibility within the community. The public information staff also write the press releases, create the library newsletter, and send mailings to patrons, the local schools, and local businesses and organizations. The fifth member represents your library foundation. This is a non-profit organization that supports library services through fund-raising events, such as book sales.

The five members of this committee were chosen very deliberately. The reference/adult, children's, and young adult specialists are members for obvious reasons. They work closely with your patrons. They see what materials adults, children, and young adults are using, and they hear their questions. They will have a good feel for what programs will and won't fly for various age groups. And, they can communicate with their peers throughout the library (and perhaps throughout the profession, if they have access to e-mail).

The member from your public information office (or your communications office or graphics office) will be an important asset. This person will know what local or national events are occurring, such as arts or music festivals, and they can help you tie programming ideas into such events. For example, the best time to do a program on bicycling might be during National Bike Month in May. This member will also be able to tell the committee when it is overextending itself. Your library can adequately promote only a certain number of programs in the local newspapers and other media. This person will also have a good feel for how your patrons may react to certain programs or presenters. Will hiring an investment broker from Best Bank to give a talk on stocks offend the brokers from the other banks around town? Your public information office might be able to provide some insight.

The representative from your library foundation—and let's just assume you have such a foundation—is invaluable. Your library foundation will hopefully have funds at its disposal and, if it is affiliated with your Friends group, might have volunteers as well. By including the library foundation on your committee, ideally you will find that the foundation will offer to pay for and produce (with the help of the Friends' volunteers) certain programs. The foundation will benefit because you will credit it in the program's publicity. Add a "Presented by the Alakazam Library Foundation" byline to the flyers and press releases. Library foundations also frequently fund such events as gala openings for new library buildings. The brainstorming that takes place in your programming committee meetings can help foundations locate performers for such events.

Now that you have all your members in attendance and you've discussed this month's programming calendar, it's time to proceed with the meeting. You might be wondering why you are here. The primary function of this committee is to act as a clearinghouse for programming in the library. You look at the agenda for today's meeting and see that the only business is the discussion and approval of programs. The best way to visualize how this committee functions is to look at how programming ideas and information travel through your library system.

Anyone in the library can submit a program idea. This idea goes to the chair of the program committee—you. Ideas also trickle in through patron suggestions on the program evaluation forms. (Please see chapter 12 for detailed information on evaluating programs.) Each branch also has one or two "programming representatives," preferably someone from the children's room and someone from the reference/adult services room. These representatives are expected to be very active in recommending topics and performers. Depending on the size of your library, this group of programming representatives could be fairly large. Ideally, they will be able to communicate with the program committee and among themselves via e-mail.

The first items you discuss are the programming ideas. These are rough ideas and suggestions that come to the chair through staff and patrons. You will also receive proposals from members of your community who want to speak at the library. Patron suggestions are often as simple as "have a program on travel in Europe." The committee encourages staff to try to flesh out ideas before they send them to the committee. When possible, the committee asks that the following be included when staff submit an idea:

- The topic of the program
- The name of a performer who might be able to present a program on that topic
- The content of the program
- The length of the program
- The cost of the program
- The months of the year that the performer is available
- Whether the performer is available to appear at other branches throughout the library system
- Whether the performer has appeared at other libraries or made other local appearances

The committee then discusses the idea. The committee first decides whether the proposed program ties into the library's mission. If someone suggests "a night of disco dancing," does this mesh with your program policy and mission statement? You look carefully at who the performers are and how they present themselves. Does the World War II historian present himself in his cover letter to the library as "Bart of Bart's World War II Emporium"? You might choose to go with Bart, but you will probably want to speak with

him first about the amount of publicity he can give his shop during his lecture. You might want to call performers' references.

Your public information representative will help you decide in which month to place the program. If the library is gearing up to massively publicize the children's and young adult summer reading program in June and July, then it might be too much to try to publicize two adult program series in June. Or, the public information office might have insight into the current concerns of your patrons. For example, this office fields many of the calls that the library receives from the public. If staff have received twenty-five calls in one month from patrons who don't approve of your library's Internet access policy, they might tell you that now isn't the best time to present a workshop entitled "Romance and Maybe More on the Internet."

Committee members like the first idea they discuss and decide to proceed: A programming representative in one of the branches has proposed that the library hire a local author who has written a book on natural hot springs. You see that the performer is asking $100 per appearance. You check the programming budget and see that the money is there to fund the program. You then check the programming calendar, where you track all the pending programs, and see that November seems relatively clear. November makes sense: Your library is in Colorado; November is the beginning of the ski season; and people like to relax in a hot spring after a full day of skiing. You all agree that you would like to offer this program in at least three branches. You, as chair, ask someone on the committee to present this approved concept to the branch representatives.

At this point the committee is looking for one of the programming representatives in the branches to coordinate the hot springs program. The committee either faxes, e-mails, or mails a memo to the programming representatives asking for a volunteer. Hopefully one of the representatives will step forward and offer to coordinate the program. This coordinator will call the performer, get days and times that she can appear at the library, verify whether she is willing to appear at more than one branch, and settle on the length of the program and the appearance fee.

The coordinator should also ask the performer to fax, mail, or e-mail an outline of what will be covered during the program. This ensures that the performer will present what you expected her to present. Also, the performer should provide a brief (two or three sentences) biographical sketch. This will help your graphics or public information office create flyers and press releases. If you plan on paying the performer and drafting a check, the coordinator will also want to get a social security number.

The coordinator will then solicit other branches to see if they would also like to offer this program. This is an effective way to make quality programs available to all the branches. This means that each branch doesn't have to think up its own ideas and seek out its own performers.

Here's how the hot springs concept will be presented to the branches. The coordinator will present the idea to the branch programming representatives. The quickest way to do this is via e-mail. It can also be done via fax or interoffice memo. The coordinator sends this message to the programming representatives:

Hello. Attached you will find copies of a letter and a brochure that Brooke Springs sent the Program Committee describing the hot springs lecture she offers. Ms. Springs has published two books on Western hot springs, both of which appear in our collection. The lecture would be 90 minutes long. She would charge $100 per appearance. The workshops would take place in November. She is available on Saturdays, weekday afternoons, and evenings after 6 P.M. She would like to be scheduled no more than two evenings during this series. She will need a screen for her workshop; let me know if you need a screen and I will submit an AV request for you.

Ms. Springs is permitted to sell her books after her program.

Please respond to me by Monday, February 28 if you would like to host this program.

Thank you.

Donna Smith
Green Lawn Branch

The library representatives then check their branch calendars and consult with their library managers and then let the program coordinator know if they are willing/able to host the program. When the coordinator has heard back from all the representatives, he calls the performer and verifies the selected days and times. Then the coordinator begins submitting the necessary paperwork.

Handling Paperwork

Two types of forms are fairly common in libraries: a program request worksheet and a graphics request. The program request (fig. 2.3) would go to a program committee or to a systemwide coordinator, such as the head of adult services. This sheet lists the performer's information needed by the accounting office to draft a check. It also verifies the locations where the performer will appear, and it contains information about the program itself, such as the title and the type of publicity you are requesting. Accompanying information about the performer, such as the biographical sketch, would be stapled to this request to help staff create the flyers and press releases. The graphics request (fig. 2.4) specifies the type of publicity you are seeking and the numbers of flyers and other items for distribution.

Planning Ahead

The process of establishing a committee may seem overly complicated, but it actually does save time by creating a program clearinghouse for the entire library system. Programming is a multidepartmental endeavor. A single program can include librarians, performers, graphics people, building services staff, and many others. And, in order to get everything done, you must plan ahead.

One phrase you will hear over and over again is "plan ahead." A large part of programming involves planning. Space for the program must be reserved ahead of time. Time must be set aside for writing whatever publicity you send to the newspapers. It takes time to create and print and

FIGURE 2.3
Program Request Worksheet

PROGRAM REQUEST WORKSHEET

Sign Off (dates and initials)   Budget Line _____

_____ _____ Branch Manager   Unit Cost _____ Total $ Approved _____

_____ _____ Programming Committee   ❑ Branch Funds ❑ General Programming ❑ Other _____

_____ _____ Public Information Officer   Check payable to: _____

Performer _____ Contract will be signed by: _____

Address_____City_____State_____ZIP_____

Phone_____ SS# or Tax ID_____

Theme (such as National Children's Book Week) _____

Program Title _____ Audience _____

Program Coordinator_____Branch_____Phone_____Date_____

Describe program or **attach descriptive materials for public information purposes.**

_____

_____

_____

_____

Publicity products requested: (copy will be written by Public Information Office from materials attached)

_____ library newsletter   _____ flier (for system-wide programs only)

_____ general news release   _____ other special release or product (specify) _____

Locations: Fill in dates and times of presentations. **Use boxes to number the programs in order by date.**
Please cross out branches not offering program.

❑ Arvada Library	❑ Conifer Library	❑ Evergreen Library	❑ Standley Lake Library
_____ day	_____ day	_____ day	_____ day
month date time	month date time	month date time	month date time
❑ Belmar Library	❑ Daniels Library	❑ Golden Library	❑ Wheat Ridge Library
_____ day	_____ day	_____ day	_____ day
month date time	month date time	month date time	month date time
❑ Columbine Library	❑ Edgewater Library	❑ Lakewood Library	**Meeting room reservations confirmed at:**
_____ day	_____ day	_____ day	___ BL ___ CL ___ EV
month date time	month date time	month date time	___ GN ___ LK ___ SL
			___ WR

White/Business Office   Canary/PIO   Pink/Program Chair   Goldenrod/Program Coordinator

_____
Source: Jefferson County (Colo.) Public Library

FIGURE 2.4
Graphic Arts Request

GRAPHIC ARTS
Job Request

SEND COMPLETED FORM TO: Director of Public Information

Approved by Unit Head _____ Date _____

Director of Public Information _____ Date _____

Senior Management Team member _____ Date _____

Required information

FORMS ONLY
Check one:

☐ **Revise**
___ Hold for next printing

☐ **New**

☐ **Reprint**

☐ **Discontinue***

*Attach copy of form

Distribute completed job to:

Location	Quantity
AR	
BL	
BK	
CF	
CL	
DN	
ED	
EV	
GN	
LSC	
LK	
PIO	
SL	
VI	
WR	
XT	
Supply	
Other ___	

IMPORTANT: Every piece of printed material to be ordered through Central Supplies will be assigned a number. This includes forms, bibliographies, bookmarks, undated brochures. The logo, JCPL, the number, month and year of latest revision will appear on each piece.

Dated publications such as the newsletter and fliers <u>do not require a form number</u>.

Title _____ Form No. _____ Quantity _____

PIO quantity _____ ☐ fold ☐ add web page _____

Submitted by _____ Branch ____ Phone # _____

Send proof to _____ Date submitted _____ Date needed _____

REMEMBER: Make a photo copy of your original text.
Proofread carefully
Return proof as soon as possible (call in OK or changes if deadline is near).

SPECIAL INSTRUCTIONS

☐ Staple ☐ Holepunch ☐ Fold ☐ Velobind ☐ Laminate ☐ Collate ☐ Pad

☐ Signs (attach description or use Notes below) ☐ Other _____

Notes (include any suggestions about size, color, etc.):

_____

_____

_____

_____

_____

To be completed by Graphic Arts Department only

Date job in _____ Date completed _____

Press size _____ Finished size _____ Sides _____

Paper weight _____ Paper color _____ Ink color _____

Other _____

_____

_____

Keep white copy (Unit File)   Submit: yellow & pink copy - Director, Public Information

Source: Jefferson County (Colo.) Public Library

distribute your flyers. Figure 2.5 is a checklist created by the Jefferson County (Colo.) Public Library. I include it to illustrate the amount of time and the number of people that can be involved in producing a single program. A library with twelve branches developed this checklist. The workload is dispersed across several departments. A single-branch library might not have the various departments included in this checklist, but it will still have to perform many of the same tasks. Someone will have to check the library's calendar to see that the program can be accommodated; someone will need to set up the room; someone will need to create and distribute the publicity; someone will have to set up any necessary equipment; someone will have to distribute, collect, and compile the evaluations, and so on.

The checklist acts as a timeline for the coordinator of the program. The idea phase should precede the event by about four months. This sounds terribly far in advance, but this is a fairly common timeline for programming. The people responsible for creating library publicity (public relations offices, graphics departments, etc.) generally want the information at least three months in advance to give them time to create flyers, newsletters, and news releases. It's also very likely that your program is just one of many publicity projects in the works. Plan ahead.

While we're in the mode of planning ahead, let's do a few more things. Let's start with a calendar-like projection of the coming year. What types of programs would you like to offer next year? If you have a budget, how would you like it to be distributed among these programs? When

FIGURE 2.5
Programming Checklist

Jefferson County Public Library (JCPL)
PROGRAMMING CHECKLIST

ADVANCE/ DATE DUE	TASK	RESPONSIBILITY OF

	Get a great idea
	AND THINK
	    Does the idea fit within the program guidelines?
	    Have you cleared time to work on this with your unit
	      head and the branch manager?
		You

+120 days	Take program idea to your unit head (head of children's,
	    head of reference, head of circulation, or branch manager)
	    for discussion at roundtable. Ask your program commit-
	    tee rep. for a packet.
	
	PROGRAM PACKET CONTENTS
	    ☐ Program Request Worksheet (jcpl 454)
	    ☐ Graphic Arts Request (jcpl 215)
	    ☐ AV Equipment Reservation (jcpl 725)
	    ☐ For Immediate Release (jcpl 729)
	    ☐ Library Program Report (jcpl 464)
	    ☐ Meeting Room Reservation
	    ☐ Program Evaluation (jcpl 446)
		You

+120–90 days	Unit Head takes idea to appropriate roundtable to determine branch interest.	Unit Head

+120–90 days	Initial no-promises contact with presenter. Ask for all
	    necessary information and fill in Program Request
	    Worksheet. Don't forget Social Security Number.
		Program Committee

+90 days	Programming Representative takes idea to program committee with roundtable recommendation.	Programming Representative

(Continued)

FIGURE 2.5
Programming Checklist (Cont'd)

ADVANCE/ DATE DUE	TASK	RESPONSIBILITY OF
+90–75 days	AND THINK . . . about these considerations before completing the packet: *Timing* the presentation in line with other library activities, publication of bibliographies and other support materials, probable schedule of target audiences. *Length of presentation* Estimate with presenter the length of presentation, or if several presenters, the overall length and the segment lengths. *Comfort of audience* (audibility in location, temperature, adequate space?, materials for general audience participation, special audience participation). *AV and presentation equipment* (does the speaker need a lectern? projection equipment? easels? a sound system? _____?). *Publicity strategy* Who needs to know about this presentation? What is the best way to reach them? What is the most important thing we can tell them about this presentation? (How will the presentation make their lives easier or better?)	Program Committee
+90–75 days	Reserve meeting room(s) with public services secretary (303-275-xxxx). Ask that one copy of the confirmation(s) be sent to the program coordinator, with a second copy of each confirmation to be sent to the appropriate branch manager.	Program Committee
+90–75 days	If approved, arrange with other branches. Draft program agenda, flyers, press releases, calendar entries, public service announcements, letters, etc. as appropriate. Complete packet: PROGRAM PACKET CONTENTS ☐ Checklist for Program (experimental) ☐ Program Request Worksheet (jcpl 454) ☐ Graphic Arts Request (jcpl 215) ☐ AV Equipment Reservation (jcpl 725) ☐ For Immediate Release (jcpl 729) ☐ Library Program Report (jcpl 464) ☐ Meeting Room Reservation ☐ Program Evaluation (jcpl 446)	Programming Representative
+90–75 days	Final packet is submitted to program committee for authorization of funding and/or contracting. Committee "nag" is assigned.	Programming Representative
upon authorization	Packet goes to Public Information Office (PIO).	Program Committee
+50 days	Contract goes out with letter and JCPL map. Letter asks presenter to indicate 　preferred floor plan 　preferred room setup (checklist provided) 　special AV or presentation equipment needed 　length of presentation 　preferred order of presentation	Business Office

ADVANCE/ DATE DUE	TASK	RESPONSIBILITY OF
+50 days	Prepare a list with addresses of potential attendees—not "general public." Include the types of individuals or special interest organizations that would probably not want to miss this presentation.	Program Committee
+50–45 days	Send special lists to PIO.	Program Committee
+50–45 days	Submit calendar entry to branch calendar rep. (Calendar is due on the 20th of the month 2 months prior—so an entry for March calendar needs to be to branch calendar rep by January 15th.)	Program Committee
+45 days	If speaker wants handouts copied, scrutinize for copyright issues. Point out any concerns when you check with branch manager. If OK, send one sample of each item to be copied to the PIO and a copy to each branch to be copied as needed.	Program Committee
+45 days	☐ Distribute press releases ☐ Contact print and electronic press as appropriate ☐ Notify chambers of commerce ☐ Arrange interviews if appropriate	PIO
+30 days	Check for appropriate bibliographies or other support materials; order adequate quantity from Administration.	Program Committee
+30 days	Mail flyers to press. Distribute to branches and special lists.	PIO
+30 days	Make arrangements for adequate staffing during program. Check staff scheduling with branch manager.	Program Committee
+30 days	Brief each presenter and each staff person directly involved on the program.	Program Committee
+21 days	Make tickets from branch ticket master sheet.	Program Committee
+ 7 days	Re-check branch meeting room schedule.	Program Committee
+ 7 days	Order flip charts, name tags, place cards, evaluation forms, and other supplies as necessary from Administration. Also order extra tables or chairs if necessary.	Program Committee
+ 7 days	Reconfirm speaker(s). Check that they have directions (they should have been sent a map) to program sites.	Program Committee
+ 7 days	Draft thank you note.	Program Committee
+ 7 days	Check background material. Write introduction of speaker. Pull display books and resources as appropriate. Outline your "I'd like to thank the presenter," "for more information in the library," or "read more about it" comments for the program's end.	Program Committee
+ 1 day	Check tables and chairs. Set up room or arrange to set it up, as appropriate, paying attention to other scheduled events.	Program Committee

(Continued)

FIGURE 2.5
Programming Checklist (Cont'd)

ADVANCE/ DATE DUE	TASK	RESPONSIBILITY OF
Day of the Event	☐ Make sure any equipment or special furniture you've ordered has arrived. ☐ Make sure the presenter has been contacted/confirmed for your branch. ☐ Make sure PIC, circ, pages, and other staff working that day are aware the program is going on. ☐ Make sure the room is ready. Check room arrangement—tables and chairs set up, AV, book displays, etc. Be sure evaluations are on the chairs. ☐ Greet the presenter. Ask about specific needs when (s)he arrives: e.g., glass of water, help with AV, name tags, etc. ☐ Gather tickets from patrons before starting the program. ☐ Keep occupancy (safety) limits in mind if you are not using tickets. ☐ Record attendance statistics (number of adults and children) for program committee members. ☐ Enjoy! Sometimes little things need to be done at the last moment. Be ready, willing, and able to assist presenters or audience on a moment's notice and with grace and good cheer. Monitor room during presentation: e.g., discipline, noise, other disturbances; offer any help the presenter might need. Observe the program in order to evaluate for JCPL. ☐ Clean up the room afterwards. Collect evaluation forms, and observe patron comments about the program. Exchange observations with presenter. Be sure to thank the presenter. ☐ Notify any staff concerned of program ending. ☐ Write up program evaluation form while it is fresh in your mind. Send it to the program committee.	Programming Representative
Within 7 days	Send thank you note(s).	Program Committee
Within 7 days	Compile patron evaluations on one form and send to the program committee.	Program Committee

creating this calendar you aren't worrying about who the performers will be. You are only identifying topics. Then you are guesstimating the costs, based on the number of locations that will host each program. You can either create a systemwide calendar or a branch-specific calendar. The month for each program will require some thought. You can work at this from either end: Either you have a topic in mind and you then try to find the best month in which to hold the event, or you have a vacant month and you are trying to

think of an event to host during that month. For example, looking at figure 2.6, you might already know that you want to host a wildflower program next year. People plant their flowers in late winter, and they begin thinking of taking nature walks during this time as well. So, how about March? If your December calendar is still vacant, perhaps you could find someone to give a talk on the winter sports possibilities in your state.

Creating such a calendar can keep you focused. It doesn't have to be etched in stone;

FIGURE 2.6
Programming Calendar

ADULT PROGRAMMING IN 200X

This table details how the Program Committee proposes to spend $5,000 on adult programming in 200X.

TYPE OF PROGRAM	DESCRIPTION	ESTIMATED COST PER LOCATION	COST FOR FIVE LOCATIONS	PROJECTED MONTH OF PROGRAM	TOTAL COST
Travel in Europe	Speaker will explain how to book cheap flights, find inexpensive lodging, and how to eat, entertain yourself, and shop on a tight budget.	$75	$375	January	$375
Non-fiction Workshop	Speaker will discuss the art of writing non-fiction, as well as the craft of writing a book proposal and the process of finding an agent.	$100	$500	February	$500
Roses and Colorado Wildflowers	Speaker will offer programs on Colorado wildflowers, romantic roses, and general rose culture in Colorado.	$30	$150	March	$150
Quilts	Speaker will cover the history of quilts, collecting quilts, tips on making quilts.	$50	$250	April	$250
Bird Watching Program	Speaker will instruct attendees on types of birds from Colorado and where to go to watch them.	$75	$375	May	$375
Glen Hanket: Underwear by the Roadside	Author shows slides of his twelve-month tour of U.S. spent picking up roadside litter.	$100	$500	June	$500
ESL Class	Hire teachers from an ESL organization to give an ESL course to 15–20 patrons.	$2,000	Would be held at a different location each year	July	$2,000
Colorado History	Local author and/or historian will offer a talk on Colorado History. (We are pursuing a program on historic Colorado barns.)	$75	$375	August	$375

(Continued)

FIGURE 2.6
Programming Calendar (Cont'd)

TYPE OF PROGRAM	DESCRIPTION	ESTIMATED COST PER LOCATION	COST FOR FIVE LOCATIONS	PROJECTED MONTH OF PROGRAM	TOTAL COST
Motorcycling in the Rockies	Speaker will talk about the equipment needed to cycle in the Rockies. Will also point out the best highways in Colorado for cycling.	$75	$375	September	$375
Adult Book Talk on Biographies	Hire a local professor to talk about the best biographies of recent years.	$75	$375	October	$375
Investing	Kathy Buys will give a program on investing. JCPL owns two of her books: *Invest with Confidence* and *Investment Basics for Women*.	$225	$1,125	November	$1,125
Winter Sports Other Than Skiing	Bring in a sports writer or owner of a local sporting goods store to give a talk on winter sports for the non-skier.	$75	$375	December	$375 ($6,775)

changes can be made. But it will definitely help you set goals and project your spending. This calendar is a kind of strategic plan. A plan can only help you if you intend to ask a group—such as your Friends group or library foundation—for money. Potential funders are impressed by proposals that show them what you intend to do, when you will do it, and how much it will cost. They may have suggestions, but this only verifies that you have gotten their attention and interest.

While we're busy making tables and such, I'll mention another piece of record keeping that can be very helpful. How do you intend to track the programs that you have booked? If you use a program request worksheet (similar to the one in fig. 2.3), then you will probably have a paper copy of that request somewhere. That works fairly well if you are in a one-branch system or if your branch is the only location hosting the program. However, if you are in a multibranch system, and

several locations agree to produce the program, then all the branches that booked the program will want some way to track their requests. Will each branch submit its own request for the same program, or will one person coordinate the program series for everyone with one request? If you choose the latter, then you will have a single request for multiple branches. This results in less paperwork, but how will all the branches keep track of the programs they've requested? One way is to create a central calendar or database that tracks the programs occurring within the library system. The Program Committee chair might maintain this database (see fig. 2.7). It will track which branches requested which programs, who the performer is, the title of the program, and the dates and times. You might also want to track housekeeping details, such as whether meeting rooms have been booked and who the coordinator of the program is.

FIGURE 2.7
Program Requests Database

PROGRAM COORDINATOR	DATE APPROVED			TOTAL $	PERFORMER	PROGRAM TITLE	DATE(S) AND LOCATION	MEETING ROOM CONFIRMED
	LIBRARY MANAGER	*PROGRAM COMMITTEE*	*P/O*					
Bart Smith	11/4/99	11/6/9	11/9/99	$0	Steve Stevens Student Help Center 2233 4th St. Denver, CO 80222	College Financial Aid	CF 1/15/00 1:00 CL 1/20/00 7:00 GN 1/27/00 7:30 VI 2/1/00 7:00 SL 2/8/00 7:00 LK 2/29/00 7:00	Y Y Y Y Y Y
Barbara Black	11/30/99	1/2/00	1/5/00	$15	Evergreen Staff	Discovery Day Magic	EV 2/22/00 2-7:00	Y
Sandy Sampson	12/4/99	12/8/99	12/9/99	$0	AARP Bruce Brown 303-222-3333	AARP Counseling for Taxes	CL Wed. 2/2/00–4/12/00 12:00 CF Sat. 3/4/00 10:00 & 1:00 EV Wed. 2/9/00–4/12/00 1:00 GN Tues. 2/1/00–4/1/00 6:30 LK Mon. 2/3/00–4/13/00 6:30 & Thurs. 2/3/00–4/13/00 12:00 SL Mon. 2/4/00–4/14/00 10:30 & 5:00 & Fri. 2/4/00–4/14/00 10:30 & Sat. 2/4/00–4/14/00 10:30 VI Wed. 2/4/00–4/12/00 12:30	Y Y Y Y Y Y Y

Answering the Tough Questions

As you continue to offer programs, you will encounter more and more questions that need answers. If you are an organization that stresses documentation, then you will want to answer these questions in terms of new policies. Or you might just want to answer these questions through staff training. Or you might do both. So many questions will come up, in fact, that you might want to form a committee if only to address the questions. The committee can meet (perhaps virtually via e-mail), discuss questions, and then get back to staff via e-mail, the library newsletters, or some other way. All right already, you say, what are these questions? We will address many of these in later chapters, but questions you will eventually have as a program coordinator include:

What do I do if the performer wants to alter his contract?

What do I do if the media, the performer, or a patron wants to videotape or take photographs?

How much am I willing to pay a performer? Many performers are professionals. They do amazing work and they charge amazing prices. It isn't hard to find a performer who is willing to charge $175 an hour.

How many branches can offer the same program during the same month? When does the library begin to compete against itself?

How do I conduct crowd control? If I know a program will be hugely popular, do I hand out tickets as people arrive? Do I take reservations over the phone?

Some of these questions can be addressed as written policies. Others are better answered through training. For example, many libraries have a ticket policy, but I imagine few have a "How Many Locations Are Too Much?" policy. Through training, you can teach program coordinators to judge how many locations should host a particular program. Through practice, you will begin to notice which topics and performers draw large crowds regardless of the number of locations that host the event. Over time, you can create a programming manual that addresses various programming issues. The manual might include an FAQ section and could be posted electronically as a Web page for staff reference.

Teaching Your Staff How to Produce Good Programs

I learn through training and practice. I don't always pick things up right away if you try to teach me something by handing me a manual or memo. I didn't learn to ride a bike through an article on gravity and momentum. I needed the guidance of my mom, some training wheels, and some sage advice, such as "keep pedaling or you'll fall" and "turn before you hit that tree." Adults can learn from reading, but we have better retention if we can actively participate in the training process and practice what we learn. If you can find a programming mentor or if you can become a mentor, you will learn more and you will enjoy learning. Let someone talk and walk you through the process, from start to finish—from the initial idea, through the production, and into the evaluation process. Be sure that training involves producing an actual program. Knowing that the result is a real performance will increase the desire to learn and participate.

Another training format—other than one-on-one mentoring—is the workshop. This workshop can cover all the dry things, such as paperwork and evaluation forms, and it can accentuate the better parts, such as choosing a topic and selecting a performer. Ending the workshop with a performance is a nice touch. Before the performance, one of the workshop presenters can explain how the performer was located and how long it took to organize the program, and then it's show time! A workshop might run ninety minutes with thirty minutes reserved for the performance. People from various departments can present portions of the workshop. For example, someone from your public relations or graphics office can present the material on publicity.

Here is a possible workshop outline:

I. Introduction (including a brief mention of how programming ties into the library's mission)

II. Types of programming

    A. Adult programming

    B. YA programming

    C. Children's programming

III. Getting started

    A. Getting to know your community

    B. Selecting a topic

    C. Planning the program's content: includes identifying a performer, choosing the right format, deciding on the performer's fee, etc.

IV. Understanding how publicity works (including deadlines for when to submit publicity)

V. Filling out the paperwork

VI. Producing a live program

    Homework: Each person in attendance will coordinate a program during the next year.

We've covered quite a bit in this chapter. We entered this chapter with a programming policy. We then developed policies and guidelines that enabled us to clarify our programming mission. We established a budget. We then formed a programming committee to provide leadership and to guide our programming efforts. We produced some paperwork that will help us coordinate the programming work that will be shared among various departments. We've created some tools that will help us in the planning process, such as calendars and databases that track our pending programs. And we've trained our staff in these policies and techniques. Most of the staff who receive this training are probably in public services (reference, adult, and children's librarians; circulation; etc.). They will be coordinating the programs. But before we put our training into practice, let's be sure that we have included administrative services in our plans.

3
Administrative Necessities

FOR THOSE OF US (SUCH AS MYSELF) WHO DON'T work in administrative services, it's easy to list at least one thing that this department does: write our paychecks. What else happens there? We're pretty sure that they somehow control the budget. They seem to handle the paperwork when people get hired. The supervisors of the building services staff seem to be located somewhere over there in administrative services. But what relation could administrative services staff have to programming? Perhaps they have to give us some money, but isn't that it? Well, no.

The budget *is* something that involves the folks in administrative services. Depending on your library's hierarchy, they may be responsible for your insurance, the performers' contracts, and the facilities and equipment you will need to host your program. Since the people in your administrative offices perform their duties so proficiently and, most likely, silently, it can be easy to overlook what they do. If you happen to perform these duties within your library, then you are very aware of how crucial they are.

We will look closely at budgeting in chapter 5. In this chapter, we will look at three other administrative necessities: insurance, contracts, and facilities and payments.

Insurance

Please be sure you have insurance in place before you host the "Animals That Bite for Fun!" program. Here's the main point to address: Be sure that your library's liability insurance policy includes programming as a "covered activity." Be prepared to talk and negotiate with your insurance provider to get this included. Your policy's premium may go up as a result of adding programming as an activity. If your insurance provider balks at the idea of adding programming, stand firm. You are the customer. Don't let your insurance provider drive your programming policy. Make it clear that library programming is an ingredient within your overall library mission. Give the representative a copy of your library's mission statement and programming policy. While meeting with the representative, be up front and honest about the types of programs you expect to offer. If you plan on cosponsoring a skydiving class and other extreme sporting events, tell the representative. You don't want her or him to be caught completely off guard if you ever present a claim from a program gone wrong. If you are planning a program that seems as if it has an element of danger to the audience, such as a wild animal exhibition, then call the person in administrative services who handles your insurance policy and explain the program. That person may then call the insurance company and explain the program to someone there. The result might be that the insurance company boosts the coverage on the policy for the period in which this program will occur.

You will also want to be sure that your performers do one of two things. Ideally, the performer will agree to sign an indemnity clause that states that he or she holds the library harmless from all claims and damages arising from the performer's actions. Run this clause past an attorney before you begin using it. Many performers have their own liability insurance. If this is the case, then ask the performer to include the library as an additional insured on the policy. Ask for proof of this insurance. Figure 3.1 is a policy for a performer, John the Juggler. In the bottom, left-hand corner labeled "certificate holder," you can see that John has included the library as an additional insured.

Contracts

You will want to provide a written agreement—a contract—to the performer. The most important thing about a contract is making sure that you have one. A sample contract is included in chapter 8. Have an attorney look over your contract before you put it into use. Let your attorney also look at your programming policy. This will help the attorney see what you are trying to accomplish with your contract. Ideally, you will develop a fill-in-the-blank contract that can be used with all your programs. It is important that you have the administrative processes in place that allow you to meet the terms of the contract. Be sure that the check is drafted in time. And last, give the performer a contact person that she or he can call with contract questions. Performers frequently ask if they can tweak the contract slightly. You will want to make sure that your contact peo-

ple know how to answer such questions or know to whom they can refer any questions.

Facilities and Equipment

The administrative departments within your library probably transport equipment between locations. They may also set up the rooms. They may clean the rooms, or they may contract with outside companies that do the cleaning. Regardless of which department does the work, it needs to be done before the program begins. In order for this to happen, you will need a process in place that allows the program coordinator to effectively communicate with the people who do the preceding tasks. Maybe you will do it all yourself, but if not, you will want to develop some method of communication. This will probably take the form of paperwork. Love it or hate it, paperwork is a good way to make a request and keep a record of what's been requested. If you have a form that you use when making requests from the building services staff, you can probably use the same form when requesting chairs or other equipment for your program. An example of such a form is included in figure 3.2. Figure 3.3 shows a form that can be used when requesting such equipment as slide projectors for your program. Frequently this type of equipment is located in a central facility and must be requested in advance.

Your administrative services staff are essential to the success of your program. They work within the realms of accountability and stewardship. They tend to our budgets and buildings, seeing that both are healthy and responsive to the needs of our patrons. Administrative services enhance our ability to provide quality programming in a responsible manner.

We've spent these first few chapters getting our internal policies and documents in order. Let's now look outward into the community and discover more about who our patrons are and what types of programs they prefer.

FIGURE 3.1
Performer Insurance Policy

ACORD™ CERTIFICATE OF LIABILITY INSURANCE

DATE (MM/DD/YY)
11/22/1999

PRODUCER (415)957-0600 FAX (415)957-0577	THIS CERTIFICATE IS ISSUED AS A MATTER OF INFORMATION ONLY AND CONFERS NO RIGHTS UPON THE CERTIFICATE HOLDER. THIS CERTIFICATE DOES NOT AMEND, EXTEND OR ALTER THE COVERAGE AFFORDED BY THE POLICIES BELOW.
Maroevich O'Shea & Coghlan 425 Market Street 10th Floor San Francisco, CA 94105	**COMPANIES AFFORDING COVERAGE**
Attn: **Ext:**	COMPANY A Royal Insurance Company of America
INSURED	COMPANY B Republic Indemnity
John the Juggler, Inc.	COMPANY C
	COMPANY D

COVERAGES

THIS IS TO CERTIFY THAT THE POLICIES OF INSURANCE LISTED BELOW HAVE BEEN ISSUED TO THE INSURED NAMED ABOVE FOR THE POLICY PERIOD INDICATED, NOTWITHSTANDING ANY REQUIREMENT, TERM OR CONDITION OF ANY CONTRACT OR OTHER DOCUMENT WITH RESPECT TO WHICH THIS CERTIFICATE MAY BE ISSUED OR MAY PERTAIN, THE INSURANCE AFFORDED BY THE POLICIES DESCRIBED HEREIN IS SUBJECT TO ALL THE TERMS, EXCLUSIONS AND CONDITIONS OF SUCH POLICIES. LIMITS SHOWN MAY HAVE BEEN REDUCED BY PAID CLAIMS.

CO LTR	TYPE OF INSURANCE	POLICY NUMBER	POLICY EFFECTIVE DATE (MM/DD/YY)	POLICY EXPIRATION DATE (MM/DD/YY)	LIMITS	
A	**GENERAL LIABILITY** COMMERCIAL GENERAL LIABILITY CLAIMS MADE [X] OCCUR OWNER'S & CONTRACTOR'S PROT	PSP045676	11/20/1999	11/20/2000	GENERAL AGGREGATE	$ 2,000,000
					PRODUCTS - COMP/OP AGG	$ 1,000,000
					PERSONAL & ADV INJURY	$ 1,000,000
					EACH OCCURRENCE	$ 1,000,000
					FIRE DAMAGE (Any one fire)	$ 300,000
					MED EXP (Any one person)	$ 5,000
A	**AUTOMOBILE LIABILITY** ANY AUTO ALL OWNED AUTOS [X] SCHEDULED AUTOS [X] HIRED AUTOS [X] NON-OWNED AUTOS	PST244513	11/20/1999	11/20/2000	COMBINED SINGLE LIMIT	$ 1,000,000
					BODILY INJURY (Per person)	$
					BODILY INJURY (Per accident)	$
					PROPERTY DAMAGE	$
	GARAGE LIABILITY ANY AUTO				AUTO ONLY - EA ACCIDENT	$
					OTHER THAN AUTO ONLY: EACH ACCIDENT	$
					AGGREGATE	$
A	**EXCESS LIABILITY** [X] UMBRELLA FORM OTHER THAN UMBRELLA FORM	PLA433286	11/20/1999	11/20/2000	EACH OCCURRENCE	$ 5,000,000
					AGGREGATE	$ 5,000,000
						$
B	**WORKERS COMPENSATION AND EMPLOYERS' LIABILITY** THE PROPRIETOR/ PARTNERS/EXECUTIVE OFFICERS ARE: [ ] INCL [ ] EXCL	13459203	10/01/1999	10/01/2000	[X] WC STATU-TORY LIMITS [ ] OTH-ER	
					EL EACH ACCIDENT	$ 1,000,000
					EL DISEASE - POLICY LIMIT	$ 1,000,000
					EL DISEASE - EA EMPLOYEE	$ 1,000,000
	OTHER					

DESCRIPTION OF OPERATIONS/LOCATIONS/VEHICLES/SPECIAL ITEMS
Issued as Evidence of Insurance

CERTIFICATE HOLDER	**CANCELLATION**
Jefferson County Public Library 10200 West 20th Avenue Lakewood, CO 80215	SHOULD ANY OF THE ABOVE DESCRIBED POLICIES BE CANCELLED BEFORE THE EXPIRATION DATE THEREOF, THE ISSUING COMPANY WILL ENDEAVOR TO MAIL __30__ DAYS WRITTEN NOTICE TO THE CERTIFICATE HOLDER NAMED TO THE LEFT, BUT FAILURE TO MAIL SUCH NOTICE SHALL IMPOSE NO OBLIGATION OR LIABILITY OF ANY KIND UPON THE COMPANY, ITS AGENTS OR REPRESENTATIVES. AUTHORIZED REPRESENTATIVE

ACORD 25-S (1/95)   ©ACORD CORPORATION 1988

FIGURE 3.2
Equipment Request

REQUEST FOR BUILDING MAINTENANCE/SERVICES

Unit _LK_ Unit Head _Brett Lear_ Today's Date _5/11_

Request _Please bring 20 chairs to the LK meeting room on Monday morning, May 15th, and remove them on Tuesday, May 16th._

Contact 1 _Brett_ Contact 2 _John Smith_

For Building Services use.

Priority_____

Work Order #_____ Date_____

Assigned to_____

Est. time to complete_____

Special instructions_____
_____

Other items that need attention_____
_____

Fill in, following completion:

Work hours used (include travel)_____

Materials used_____
_____
_____

Date completed_____

Accepted by_____

Submit: white and yellow copy   pink copy - Unit File

Source: Jefferson County (Colo.) Public Library

FIGURE 3.3
Audiovisual Equipment Request

AUDIOVISUAL EQUIPMENT RESERVATION/CONFIRMATION REPORT

1. PLEASE VERIFY THIS INFORMATION REGARDING THE AV EQUIPMENT YOU HAVE REQUESTED.
2. CALL THE PUBLIC INFORMATION OFFICE (X216) IF YOU SEE ANY MISTAKES OR HAVE ANY QUESTIONS.
3. <u>PLEASE COMPLETE THE BOTTOM OF THIS FORM AFTER USING EQUIPMENT AND RETURN IT WITH THE EQUIPMENT.</u>

Date Needed _____ - _____ - _____   **Time** _____ A.M. _____ P.M.

Equipment Borrowed   From

_____   _____

_____   _____

_____   _____

_____   _____

_____   _____

_____

Borrower's Name _____

What is the Event _____

Event's Location _____

Reserved on this date _____

Equipment must be returned to _____ **by**

Date _____ - _____ - _____   **Time** _____ A.M. _____ P.M.

PLEASE PROVIDE THE INFORMATION REQUESTED BELOW

Condition of returned equipment (circle one)

  A-OK   Needs Maintenance   Non-functional

Describe any problems you had with this equipment _____

_____

_____

_____

Signature _____   Telephone Extension _____

Submit: **white, yellow** and **pink** copies/PIO
goldenrod copy/Unit

Source: Jefferson County (Colo.) Public Library

4

Getting to Know Your Community

FRANKLY, I HEAR THE WORD *DEMOGRAPHICS* AND I groan and then grow limp. I picture myself with a stack of books filled with columns of numbers. Then I picture myself poring through these books, pulling out numbers, and plugging these same numbers into a table I'm creating on my PC. And, of course, the work is compounded by the fact that I'm far from expert on the particular software program I'm using. So, not only is the work boring, grueling, perhaps even depressing, but it's infuriating as well, as I split cells and add columns and accidentally delete entire rows instead.

Tuggle and Heller's *Grand Schemes and Nitty-Gritty Details: Library PR That Works* does a nice job of winnowing the demographic process.[1] The authors state that you should first identify the community need. You should then be sure that you have evidence of this need. Next, you investigate what efforts are being made to meet this need. And last, you decide what, if anything, the library should do to meet this need.

Needs assessments, demographic studies, surveys, marketing research—whatever you call your process of discovering who your community is and what it wants—can resemble a scavenger hunt if not done with some planning and foresight. Actually, this isn't a fair analogy. In a scav-

enger hunt, you may spend hours looking for various things, and ultimately you end up with a button, a broken shoelace, a Popsicle stick, and a used-up roll of toothpaste. After they've been collected, these items aren't very useful. But the process of locating them is challenging and fun. Needs assessments, to the nondemographer, are challenging and not so much fun. Your needs assessment should be the anti-scavenger hunt: a challenging process that yields useful results.

Begin by Asking "Why?"

Before you begin analyzing or creating studies and surveys, ask yourself this question: Why do people attend library programs? This will help focus your energies when it comes time to begin your demographic work. (If you have never offered adult programs at your library, then it will be difficult to answer this question.) Some of us have been offering programs for a while now, but we've done it in a trial-and-error fashion that's been, surprisingly, more hit than miss. But now you are ready to begin programming in a more systematic way: You'd like to get to know a little bit more about your patrons and what they want. By exploring why your patrons attend programs, you learn about who these people are. For example, you can learn quite a bit about why people attend programs by reading the comments on the program evaluation forms. People will often leave specific comments, such as "This program gave me an opportunity to share my opinions with others." Another surefire approach is to simply observe who walks into your programs. It's also okay to talk to people as they exit. Ask them what they thought, and follow up with, "What did (or didn't) you like about it?"

You can learn something about why people attend programs by noting which programs are well attended. Do your patrons flock to programs that teach them about herbal medicine or computers or health care? Do others appreciate your ability to bring big-name authors and artists into their library? Does your evaluation form ask people if they regularly use the library? Do you get the sense that your audiences view your library as a community center and attend programs here rather than attending a local organization that offers similar programs? What age groups seem to attend programs? Does it depend on the subject?

Let us say that you estimate that over half of your adult audiences attend programs to obtain information on issues and topics of interest to them, such as nutritional programs and workshops on buying a home computer. Your audiences don't seem as enthusiastic about the recreational and cultural programs—the musical events and poetry readings are poorly attended. And many audience members say they attend the events at the library because it is convenient for them—many of them are seniors and the library is in their neighborhood, within walking distance. You've not only just learned a lot more about why people attend your programs—you've also learned more about who attends. With this information, you can decide to go in at least two directions. You might decide to focus on what you are already doing well—serving seniors—and begin investigating further the makeup of your senior population. You would do this to learn more about them, which will help you tailor future programs to their wants and needs. Or you might decide to investigate the overall makeup of your community, intent on uncovering those populations that are not currently taking advantage of your programming efforts. In which direction do you look?

Focus Your Search

Before you begin your studies, be sure you know what you are looking for and why. It's best to begin by asking yourself the following question: Why am I doing this study? Is your library just beginning to offer adult programming? Did you approach your library administrators with a program proposal and they asked: Do any of our patrons even *want* adult programming? If this question was posed to you, then you will want to conduct a study that seeks to find out whether your patrons desire library programming for adults. You might want to focus on the patrons who visit the library. An in-house survey will probably provide you with the answer to your question. Surveys do not need to be long, elaborate, confusing questionnaires.

Look within Your Library

Your library might have already conducted an extensive (though not necessarily confusing) patron-satisfaction survey in recent years. Many libraries conduct surveys, such as the customer satisfaction survey created by Dr. George D'Elia.[2] Sometimes libraries conduct these surveys when they are gearing up for a mill levy campaign as a way to find out what services voters would be willing to support with their tax money. The survey might ask how high voters rank the importance of such library services as patron education classes.

Large-scale surveys and marketing studies are very labor intensive and, therefore, expensive. If your library goes down this road, it is probably at the request of the library board. A marketing firm has probably been hired. It's not likely that this effort was undertaken to gather programming data, but that doesn't mean the data won't be invaluable to you as a program planner. Check with your library manager or public relations office to see what surveys your library has conducted, and ask permission to view the survey and the results. These data will likely contain information on satisfaction levels with particular library services, languages spoken in the community, and types of businesses within the community. And, if a marketing firm was hired, the data will be massaged into tables, graphs, and bulleted lists. Recommendations will be included in the report. The report might state that there is a need for English as a Second Language (ESL) resources and services. Or, it might reveal that seniors make up a large percentage of the population and yet do not frequently visit the library. This information quickly gives you ideas for ESL classes and programs cosponsored by the American Association of Retired Persons (AARP), such as income tax assistance for seniors.

Your library probably already has other types of information that will be helpful to you. Libraries that have a history of programming will also have some history of statistics. These might be in a rough format. For example, your program committee might have a binder that contains the patron evaluation forms from the programs offered over the last few years. If, upon completing a program, you have to submit an evaluation form to a central office, such as the Office of Adult Services, then that office might have a file of past programs that you can look at. Statistics such as these will give you an idea of the popularity of the various topics offered in the past. If your evaluation forms ask patrons to recommend future programs, you will gain insight into additional programming possibilities.

Look at State and National Resources

Your library very likely submits reports to your state library. These reports may be available via the Web. You might also have copies of the reports in your collection. It isn't unusual for these reports to contain information on the number of programs that were offered in a given year, the attendance, and the attendance per capita. Ask around to determine which organizations your library cooperates with. Does your library complete surveys sent to it from the American Library Association or the Public Library Association? For example, a publication called the *Statistical Report* compiles statistical data from the Public Library Data Service (PLDS) survey.[3] PLDS receives its funding through the Public Library Association. The *Statistical Report* does contain information on library programs.

The Federal-State Cooperative System for Public Library Data (FSCS) also distributes a survey to public libraries. The FSCS is a government program funded by the National Center for Education Statistics (NCES). The NCES Web site (nces.ed.gov/surveys/libraries/) allows you to compare your library (if you completed an FSCS survey) to other libraries. The Web site will even create a graph to illustrate the comparisons. The graph in figure 4.1 was created on the Web site and compares New York Public Library (the "library of interest") to Brooklyn Public Library and Queens Borough Public Library (the "peer group"). Currently, the FSCS survey does not collect data on adult programs. However, the NCES is working on a survey for adult programming.

FIGURE 4.1
NCES Library Comparison Graph

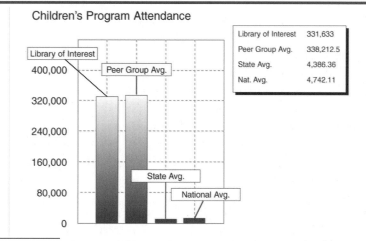

Source: National Center for Education Statistics, Library Statistics Program (Washington, D.C.: National Center for Education Statistics, n.d.), http://nces.ed.gov/surveys/libraries/publicpeer/.

As you can see, there are several state and national surveys floating around out there. The point is that your library may already be collecting and submitting information that can help you determine the number of people who are attending programs within your organization. These reports will also contain information about your patrons, such as age ranges, income levels, and educational backgrounds. Your library might have copies of the reports and surveys it has submitted in recent years. Ask. Also ask if these reports and surveys were compiled and published. It is often easier to read a finished product, such as the *Statistical Report,* than it is to read an individual report or survey. And, the compiled publication will usually place your results alongside those of other, similar libraries.

Learn How to Look

By now it's becoming clear that there is quite a bit of information out there, and it's located in a number of places. Even if you have determined what you are looking for, you may still be overwhelmed as you begin your search. The American Library Association has published a manual called *Planning and Role Setting for Public Libraries.*[4] One of the chapters, titled "Looking Around," addresses how librarians can gather information about their library and community. One of the sections in this chapter

explains how to "prepare for looking around." This is a good point, because the information you seek will determine where you need to look. Before you get too involved in your search, spend some time thinking about where you will look. For example, the manual explains that if you want to gather information on the age of your community members, you could use the *County and City Data Book.*[5] If you want to determine the number of registered borrowers or the number of adults that check out materials, then your library's own records are the place to look. And, surveys can tell you how familiar the community is with the services you offer.

Develop a Community Profile

Eventually, you will want to learn some specific things about your community that won't be included in the sources mentioned earlier. A good first step is to sketch out a basic profile of your community. Ask yourself questions that will help you define your community. In their manual *Planning Library Programs,* Peggy O'Donnell and Patsy Read provide a survey (see fig. 4.2) for conducting a quick community profile.[6] This survey is designed to help you gather information about your community. In addition, *Planning for Results: A Public Library Transformation Process: The How-To Manual* contains a chapter called "Scan the Community."[7] The manual also contains an

FIGURE 4.2
Community Survey

You can develop a profile of your community using the following questions as guidelines. Include any additional information you think is pertinent.

What are the major businesses or industries?

What dominant groups make the population?

What are the ages and characteristics of the population?

What leisure time activities are available?

What is the general education level of the population?

What economic, social, or political trends are presently affecting people in your town?

What is the town's relation to other communities in the state?

What is the historical background?

What are the present economic conditions?

What are the major cultural and religious influences?

Source: Peggy O'Donnell and Patsy Read, *Planning Library Programs* (Chicago: Public Library Association, 1979), 12.

excellent worksheet that you can use when gathering demographic information. The recently published *New Planning for Results* also contains a chapter on identifying community needs, "Imagine: Identifying Possibilities."[8]

As you begin your community scan, especially if you are new to your community, you might want to devote some time to doing something that seems obvious—reading the newspaper. The newspaper will give you a feel for who is in your community and what their interests are. A newspaper will certainly help you answer some of the questions posed in figure 4.2. The newspaper is a great tool for quick demographic information. Another simple approach is to take a walk. Stroll around your neighborhood and take in the people you see and what they are doing. Listen to them speak. Do you notice any languages other than English? What types of businesses do you see in the area? Who seems to live in the houses and apartments? Do you notice pockets of seniors or twenty-somethings? At the very least, a walk will give you a broader perspective on the people you serve and where they come from.

Ask Others for Help

Once you have a better feel for your community, you will better know which additional questions to ask. Perhaps you've identified the leisure activities available in your community, but now you want to know which activities are the most popular. If your library hasn't conducted any significant studies, you can ask other agencies and groups for help. Groups that serve most or all of the community frequently conduct demographic studies. School systems, chambers of commerce, radio stations, newspapers, and organizations serving specific populations (such as the AARP) all conduct demographic work. Ask them if they will share this information with you.

Other libraries might be able to help. Have other systems with community profiles similar to yours conducted surveys? If you have e-mail access, you could hop onto an electronic discussion group such as *PUBLIB* and post this question.[9] You could post a description of your community and ask if any libraries with similar communities have conducted surveys. Ask if

they will share their results with you. Some library, somewhere, has conducted a survey that asks the same questions that you would like to ask your patrons. Are you curious about your senior population and their interests? Perhaps another library, with a similar clientele, has asked seniors what their favorite leisure activities are. By reviewing the answers given by another library's patrons, you might learn more about your own community.

Another possibility is to seek out published library surveys and see if any of the findings seem applicable to your library and community. For example, *Cultural Programs for Adults in Public Libraries* found that the presence of a strong cultural community influenced the types of programs offered by the libraries within the community.[10] It seems that libraries were able to offer successful cultural programs when the libraries were located in communities whose residents were active in music, poetry, film, and so on. This is an interesting finding, because we are often reluctant to offer programs in areas where we feel we might be competing with agencies that are already providing this service. If your library serves an area that is strong in the arts, it seems that people will attend your programs, even if you are complementing or duplicating events that are currently available in your community.

Conduct a Survey: Ask Your Patrons What They Want

Although the strategies above can offer insight into your community, ideally you will be able to pose questions to your own patrons. Again, check to see if your library has conducted a survey that would help you with planning programs. If you discover that no survey has been conducted recently that addresses library programming, then you may have to create a survey. Even if your library has been offering programs for quite some time, it can't hurt to take another look at your community. And it never hurts to ask your patrons what they want and need, even if they have been asked before. Some of your patrons will write "Thanks for asking!" on the survey.

You can frequently get the answers you need with a brief postcard survey. Actually, a survey in the form of a postage-paid postcard works well. It gives patrons the option of taking the survey home, completing it at another time, and mailing it in to ensure anonymity. Short surveys are a good way to get the answer to yes or no questions. If you want to ask your adult patrons if they would attend adult programs, try a survey. Before you print the postcards and hand them out to your patrons, however, ask yourself if you just want a yes or a no for an answer. People will almost always say yes if you ask them if they'd like an additional, free service. The survey can be written in a way that makes the patron make a choice, thereby providing you with more useful information. For example, instead of merely asking "Would you attend adult programs if they were offered at your local library?," you might develop a survey similar to that in figure 4.3.

More people will fill out a brief survey than will struggle through a five-page monster. How much is enough? Try to think of what you will and could do with the results. The sample survey in figure 4.3 is good if you want to know what your patrons in general would like. But if you later decide that you'd like to offer more programs for seniors, this survey won't help you much. You could add a line that asks the respondent to check an age range: under 17, 17 to 25, 25 to 40, 40 to 55, 55 or older. You could then use the results to get programming ideas for particular age groups.

Surveys can be time-consuming. To obtain a fairly low percentage of error—about 3 percent—on a survey, you will need to ask about one thousand people. This is true even if your community's population is around ten thousand. I'm no statistician, so I grabbed a copy of *Statistics the Easy Way* by Douglas Downing and Jeffrey Clark. The authors, in lay terms, tell me that "a sample of 1,000 does just as well when the population is 200 million as it does when the population is 50,000. You might expect that the sample would become less accurate as the population becomes larger, but it doesn't work that way." [11]

Ideally, you would hire a marketing firm to construct your survey, determine your sample population, and tabulate the results. In reality, this is probably outside your financial capabilities. The next best thing is to find a survey that seems to ask the questions you want answered. For example, *Library Programs: How to Select, Plan, and Produce Them* by John S. Robotham and Lydia LaFleur contains some good examples of programming-related surveys.[12]

Once you have your survey ready, it's time to decide how to distribute the survey and who your sample will be. Will you conduct the survey via phone? Who will you call? Library patrons with

FIGURE 4.3
Programming Survey

If we were to begin offering adult programs, which type of program would you be most likely to attend? Please select one of the following:

_____ A monthly book discussion group

_____ A film series covering a theme, such as "Great Silent Classics" or "Film Noir"

_____ A "how to" program, such as "How to Select a Home Computer" or "How to Travel Cheap in Europe"

_____ A speaker sharing his or her knowledge with the audience; for example, a Holocaust survivor recounting her experiences at Auschwitz

_____ Workshops or classes that explain how to use library resources, such as the Internet and the online magazine index

_____ I do not have an interest in attending library programs for adults.

Comments:

library cards? Registered voters? Calling one thousand people can be time-consuming and costly. The most cost-effective way to conduct the survey is to keep it short and hand it out to folks in some public area. Include a postage-paid envelope, or place the survey on the back of a postage-paid postcard. If you're unable to pay the postage on the survey, ask people if they can take a few moments to fill it out. Otherwise, many people will take the survey from you, keep walking, and deposit it in the nearest trash can.

Where you distribute the survey determines what population you are surveying. If you survey people in the mall, you are definitely surveying mall users, but you might not be surveying library users. This is fine, particularly if you are trying to discover what additional services—such as programming—might get new patrons into the library. But, if you want to see what new services your library patrons might be interested in, then you should probably hand out the survey inside the library. This method taps into most of your library patrons—but not all. Many libraries deliver books to the homebound and to nursing homes. Let's assume that your library delivers books to several nursing homes, and you would like to begin offering some outreach programming—short-story discussion groups—to the residents. You won't be able to survey these seniors at the library, so you might want to mail the surveys to a contact person at the nursing home and ask him or her to distribute, collect, and mail the surveys back to you.

Perhaps you are trying to attract more seniors or small-business owners or college-age teens to the library. You've heard that teens really seem to love poetry contests. A teen poetry contest might bring young adults into your library for the first time. What else might work? You could write a survey—tailored to teens—that asks for programming suggestions. But you don't have many teens walking into your library. The best approach will be to take the survey to them. You could ask a teacher in a nearby school if you could speak before the class for five minutes to explain that your library is seeking input from teens on potential library programs. Then distribute and collect the survey. Or, you could ask a local newspaper that is popular with teens to insert a self-addressed, postage-paid survey into the next issue.

With certain exceptions, the library is a great place to survey library patrons. Can the survey be handed out to patrons in any section of the building? Should you give the survey to all your patrons? It depends on the intent of the survey. If you are asking people what adult programs they would want to see produced, should you give the survey to children and teens? Recently, we conducted a customer satisfaction survey of patrons in the Jefferson County (Colo.) Public Library. The questionnaire asked patrons if they were able to locate the materials they sought, and, if not, what types of materials were lacking. We realized that we should *not* distribute the survey at the checkout desk, because people checking out books probably *did* find something they wanted. We distributed the survey as people left the library, thereby including both the satisfied and perhaps not-so-satisfied patrons.

In their book, Robotham and LaFleur include a chapter on publicity. They mention that a library's mailing list can be used to disseminate information. The authors give an example (see fig. 4.4) of a stamped, self-addressed postcard that

FIGURE 4.4
Postcard Survey

Dear Library User,

The Klondike Public Library is updating its mailing list. If you wish to continue receiving announcements of programs and other library mail, please fill in the postcard and drop it in the mail box, or bring it with you when you next come to the library.

Name: _____

Address: _____

Organization you represent (if any): _____

_____

Kinds of programs that interest you: _____

_____

Source: John S. Robotham and Lydia LaFleur, *Library Programs: How to Select, Plan, and Produce Them,* 2nd ed. (Metuchen, N.J.: Scarecrow, 1981), 275.

could be included with the newsletter or program flyers that you send to people on your mailing list.[13] Although the card's main intent is to update the mailing list, it also asks respondents about their programming preferences.

The information you gather from your surveys and other demographic work will allow you to better tie programming to the library's mission and its goals. You will be able to tie programming to your mission because you will know who the people in your community are, and you will know what they want and need. Unlike your mission, your library's goals might change to a fairly large extent from year to year. Here is an example: Your library has decided to go to the voters for a mill levy increase in the fall. A study of your patron database has shown that 60 percent of the people who have checked out a book in the last year are between the ages of 24 and 44. The library board wants the library to continue to provide excellent materials and services to this age range to ensure that they are on board when they go to the polls in November. The library begins pursuing various courses of action. You are asked to plan some programs that will appeal to this age group. At first you panic because you can't imagine what consensus a group of people between the ages of 24 and 44 could ever reach on programming preferences. The beads of sweat on your brow evaporate, however, when you realize that a recent postcard survey asked patrons about their program preferences *and* their age. You can now analyze the results and see if any common threads exist for the 24 to 44 age range. You're on your way to creating great programs, targeting 60 percent of your patrons, and winning the mill levy campaign!

times learn things that surprise us. This will be true of your demographic work. You do run the risk of discovering that what you thought to be true is false. Perhaps you never geared any programs toward low-income families because you were sure that your library sat within an affluent county. Yet your research shows that the family income for 40 percent of the families in the county is less than $50,000 a year. You don't have people asking for books in other languages at the information desk, yet data supplied by the public school system show that 30 percent of the children enrolled in primary school have parents who do not speak English. What do you do with this information?

You can do at least three things with "new" information. First, you can file it (i.e., ignore it). This makes seeking information rather pointless, but it is an option. Second, you can use the information to set new goals. One of your programming goals for next year could be to offer programs to assist low-income families. For example, you might offer a program on college financial aid and a program on job hunting. These programs might benefit families concerned about whether they can afford to send their children to college and patrons who are thinking about pursuing a different career path. These programs fit within your library's mission. But, what if you decide to offer English as a Second Language (ESL) classes or literacy classes? Has your library ever done this before? If not, you might find that your administration will ask for a bit of justification before you are permitted to offer the first six-week ESL course in the library. This brings us to the third thing you can do with demographic information: Use it to write a proposal.

What Do You Do with This Information?

Information is wonderful. We usually seek it to verify what we think we know or to find out what we don't. We are frequently relieved when we find a piece of information that confirms what we already suspected to be true. But seeking the answers to questions is an adventure. We some-

Program Proposals

An in-house proposal is quite different from a proposal you would submit to a potential funding source, such as the National Endowment for the Humanities. In-house proposals usually take the form of a memo. In *Proposal Writing: The Art of Friendly Persuasion,* William S. Pfeiffer offers step-by-step advice on how to write a memo proposal.[14] Pfeiffer explains that the proposal should be written as a memo, with the standard "date," "to," "from," and "subject" lines. Since the purpose of this memo is to persuade library administrators to make changes or to try something new, the memo should be sensitive to the political climate of the organization. This means that you should think before you write, and you should share your memo with others before you submit it. If you were to pore over several successful memo proposals that have been submitted within your library over the years, you would probably discover that they contain a similar tone and format. Every library system also has a phrase or concept that is anathema to the powers that be. For example, perhaps your library director has spent many board meetings educating the library board on the fact that volunteers are not interchangeable with librarians. You have an idea about how volunteers can assist librarians with data entry projects, such as inputting obituary notices into your obit database. Present this very carefully and explicitly. You might not want to write "Volunteers Relieving Librarians of Duties" in the subject line.

Your memo can be up to five pages in length. Write the memo in a way that grabs and maintains the reader's interest. Use a subject that immediately hints at how the proposal will benefit the library. For example, you might write "Effective Use of Volunteers in Data Entry Projects." This shows that you have an idea that is going to focus on getting things done—being effective—without putting librarians out of a job. The opening paragraph should summarize the proposal. Next, include a section that shows why there is a need to go in your suggested direction. You could explain your library's current staffing situation. Then you could describe how beneficial an obituary database would be to your patrons. But, you explain, the current staffing situation permits the project to advance only at an extremely slow pace. Data entry is not a primary job duty of any of your staff—librarians, clerks, and pages included. By recruiting volunteers, you could complete a project without infringing on the job duties of any of your staff.

The main body of your proposal will contain the details. This section would explain how you intend to recruit and train the volunteers. This is also the place to state why this proposal is the right thing to do. You can include a bulleted list of benefits that will result from having the volunteers perform this data entry. These points should be as patron-focused as possible. Include such points as:

> The database will be available to our patrons in two months, instead of six.
>
> Librarians will be able to transfer their energies from data entry to creating bibliographies and developing patron-training classes.

Proposal writing is a fairly political endeavor, and it doesn't hurt to think politically as you write. If your library is currently conducting a publicity campaign to attract seniors, it might be wise to mention the number of seniors who request obituary notices each month. State that this database will allow the library to better serve these seniors. In your conclusion, summarize the proposal and emphasize a major benefit. Why should the reader give this a try? Perhaps you can stress that this proposal will allow you to quickly develop an additional service for your patrons without diminishing your staff's ability to offer excellent information assistance while the database is being developed. Don't forget to keep the memo itself under five pages. You can always add statistical tables and other items as attachments. Graphics do catch the eye, so a relevant chart or graph will accentuate your main points. And remember, before you place the proposal in interoffice mail, pause, proofread it, and ask a coworker to proofread it as well. Then send it off and watch yourself become a catalyst for change!

By now, you have all kinds of ideas. The community data you gathered tell you who is in your community, and you have ideas on how you can serve them through programming. You might have even asked your patrons what they want directly through a survey. Or you might have just been given the green light to go ahead with that area of programming (such as ESL classes) that you proposed to your library administration. Basically, we are ripe with ideas. We have our road atlas out, we've planned our trip, and we know where we want to go. Let's make sure our gas tank is full. In other words, let's check to see that our programming coffers are flush with funds.

Endnotes

1. Ann Montgomery Tuggle and Dawn Hansen Heller, *Grand Schemes and Nitty-Gritty Details: Library PR That Works* (Littleton, Colo.: Libraries Unlimited, 1987), 37.

2. George D'Elia, *The Roles of the Public Library in Society: The Result of a National Survey: Final Report* (Evanston, Ill.: Urban Libraries Council, 1993), 225.

3. Public Library Association, *Statistical Report '93: Public Library Data Service* (Chicago: Public Library Association, 1993).

4. Charles R. McClure and others, *Planning and Role Setting for Public Libraries: A Manual of Options and Procedures* (Chicago: American Library Association, 1987).

5. Bureau of the Census, *County and City Data Book: A Statistical Abstract Supplement* (Washington, D.C., published annually).

6. Peggy O'Donnell and Patsy Read, *Planning Library Programs* (Chicago: Public Library Association, 1979).

7. Ethel Himmel and William James Wilson with the ReVision Committee of the Public Library Association, *Planning for Results: A Public Library Transformation Process: The How-To Manual* (Chicago: American Library Association, 1998), 37, G-1.

8. Sandra S. Nelson for the Public Library Association, *The New Planning for Results: A Streamlined Approach* (Chicago: American Library Association, 2001), 41.

9. University of California Regents, *PUBLIB and PUBLIB-NET Electronic Discussions: General Information* (Berkeley, Calif.: SunSITE, 1997), http://sunsite.berkeley.edu/PubLib/.

10. Debra Wilcox Johnson, *Cultural Programs for Adults in Public Libraries: A Survey Report* (Chicago: American Library Association, 1999).

11. Douglas Downing and Jeffrey Clark, *Statistics the Easy Way*, 3rd ed. (Hauppauge, N.Y.: Barron's, 1997), 233.

12. John S. Robotham and Lydia LaFleur, *Library Programs: How to Select, Plan, and Produce Them*, 2nd ed. (Metuchen, N.J.: Scarecrow, 1981).

13. Ibid.

14. William S. Pfeiffer and Charles H. Keller Jr., *Proposal Writing: The Art of Persuasion* (Upper Saddle River, N.J.: Prentice-Hall, 2000), 226–35.

5
Getting Funded

LIBRARIES CAN OFFER TERRIFIC PROGRAMS WITHOUT any direct dollar costs. Excellent performers can be readily found who will offer their services to libraries for free. Museums, universities, associations, and businesses will all supply performers at no cost. A large percentage of the professional performers who charge a fee can be hired for $25 to $50 an hour. Until your library really gets its programming effort wound up to a high pitch, you probably won't be spending a great deal of money on performer's fees.

In-Kind Expenses

Initially, expenses will arise through the in-kind support you provide. In-kind support can include staff, meeting space, publicity, printing, and equipment. And even these expenses can be kept to a minimum. Libraries with budget constraints might limit their in-kind support to some basic publicity. A staff member can write a quick paragraph on the upcoming program and send this off to the local papers. Some papers will run such an announcement for free. Most papers will at least

run the program title, date, time, and location. This publicity might be done in conjunction with creating a flyer on your computer, posting this flyer throughout the library, and placing a stack at the checkout desk. The total in-kind expenses would be the staff time involved in planning the program, contacting the performer, and creating the publicity.

Libraries that have the resources to do so, however, will involve other departments and staff as they gain momentum with their programming. A graphics or public relations office will help with flyers and news releases, your building services department will bring additional chairs and tables to your branch, your automated resources people will wire your meeting room for Internet access so that the computer-buying guy can give a live demo. Your in-kind expenses will become your true programming expenses, and the $25 you are paying the performer will become somewhat irrelevant.

In-kind support does not normally appear in a programming budget, but it does need to be acknowledged in the planning phase. As you begin to offer more programs with better publicity, your program committee will want to look ahead at the in-kind support it will need in the coming months and years. Will your graphics department need to hire more staff and purchase more materials to meet the publicity needs? Will the library need to hire more staff to plan programs? If so, these departments will need increases in their budgets to achieve these goals. If such additional funding is not a possibility, then this will affect how you plan programs. Perhaps you do not have the staff, meeting space, and equipment necessary to produce more than one program a month.

Operating Funds

Some libraries perpetually operate without creating an adult programming budget. Since many adult programs are informational in nature, it is fairly easy to find organizations that receive their funding for sharing and disseminating information. Museums, universities, and associations will send their representatives out into the community to share their knowledge. Libraries are also adept at tapping into local businesses that will send experts to present state-of-the-art information. They do this for free because it is good PR for their businesses.

Performers who charge are usually making their living through their art. This includes the stockbroker, who frequently makes good money at her or his art. The library offers a nice venue for subtle advertising, and the stockbroker is willing to perform for free in exchange for the free publicity. The author or painter or guitar player might also exchange a free performance for the free exposure. Many performers, however, rely on public readings and art instruction opportunities and concerts for their weekly paycheck. This means that your idea for a program is their idea of work. It's work that they love, but work nonetheless. These people might justifiably ask for a small stipend. If your library administration agrees to dedicate a portion of the operating budget to hiring performers, you will want to create a line item for programming. Statistically, about one library out of four creates a separate line item in its budget for adult programming.[1]

Give Programming a Home within Your Budget

Chapter 2 discussed the importance of creating a programming budget. If your library has decided that programming is fundamental to its mission, and if the money is there, then it is imperative that a specified amount of money be placed into a specific programming budget line. This gives programming a home within your institution. By placing a dollar figure behind programming, you really etch programming into your basic operating procedures. You will want to work with your budgeting people to determine how to best create this budget. Should it be a single line item for programming, or should the budget specify dollar amounts for children's and adult and YA programming? As stated in chapter 2, you will also want to be clear on what the programming budget can pay for. Can supplies, such as glue and scissors for a crafts program, come out of this budget? Will they instead come from the supplies budget? Can you charge food for an artist's reception to the programming budget? You will find that your organization's policies and priorities determine your programming budget. Your policies will clarify the focus of your programs, and your library's goals and priorities will clarify how programming fits within the overall mission of your library.

If you are just beginning to offer programming in your library, don't be afraid to start out small and simple. The important thing is that you've got your foot in the door. Focus on your goals that come from your programming policy. Initially, request or create a budget that allows you to produce a few, high-quality programs each year. Then keep track of well-attended programs and their attendance figures and patrons' comments. If you document these successful programs, you will be in good stead if and when you decide to propose that more money be added to the budget. As Alexandre Dumas said, "Nothing succeeds like success."

When it is time to make a request to increase your programming budget, you will want to stress the successful history of your programs, and you will want to ground the proposal in the idea that programming has accentuated the library's ability to fulfill its mission. You should bullet a few points that illustrate how programming has accomplished this. Some hard statistics should be included, such as attendance figures and staff time involved in producing the programs. Before you even write the proposal, think about what you can do to create a positive buzz around programming. Positive, anecdotal information from your patrons and staff carry a lot of weight, especially with library board members. If you have engaged in partnerships with other organizations, be sure to include that information. This shows that you are engaging in resource sharing, which means that you are trying to stretch your dollars. Remember to extend your publicity to include those people and groups that determine or influence your budget. Be sure that board members and community leaders are on your publicity mailing lists. Keep programming and its successes in front of your administrators and policy makers. Try to get a brief programming report integrated into the library board report or annual report. Include statistics and anecdotes in this report and keep it very brief to ensure that it gets read. If you coordinate programs at your library or branch library, include a programming report in whatever report you submit to your supervisor each month. By making programming a known commodity, it will be a strong candidate for continued and possibly increased funding.

Seeking Additional Funding

Only about 8 percent of public libraries depend entirely on library operating funds for adult programming. Library Friends groups are the most common outside source of funding for adult programming. In fact, three out of four libraries collaborate with Friends groups. The most common contribution from these Friends groups is money. Other sources of outside funding include humanities councils and arts groups or councils.[2] Some libraries have a library foundation instead of a Friends group. Whether your library has a Friends group or a library foundation, chances are that the group has not-for-profit status to increase its capacity for fund-raising. These groups traditionally exist to support and enhance the services and resources of libraries. Most Friends groups and library foundations are governed by a steering committee. Your request for programming support will probably be submitted to this committee. The following case study shows how one library approached its library foundation for additional programming support.

▓▓▓▓▓▓▓▓ **CASE STUDY** ▓▓▓▓▓▓▓▓

The Jefferson County (Colo.) Public Library traditionally had a $10,000 budget for programming. This money came from the library's general operating budget. Over the years, this money usually paid for performers for children's programs. The adult programs were usually created and presented by staff, or performers were brought in from organizations and associations that provided them at no charge. Very little was offered in terms of YA programming. Around 1997, the library began expanding its adult programs and initiating young adult programs. This meant that more programs would be competing for the same amount of money—$10,000. In 1998, the library asked the library foundation for funds to supplement programming for that year. The library, however, did not spend all the money that the foundation granted, so the foundation allowed the library to carry the unspent money forward into the 1999 budget. Rolling money over from one year to the next isn't a great idea. It causes budgeting confusion. It can also cause the library to appear disorganized to funding sources. They may ask: "Why did you request that much money if you can't even spend it?" By the end of 1999 it became clear that it was time to seek additional funding again, but this time it needed to be done in a more strategic fashion.

The programming committee decided that the best way to request the money was to keep it simple. They decided to dedicate the entire programming budget of $10,000 (from the library's general operating budget) to adult and YA programming. Children's programming had a proven track record of excellence, so the committee decided to ask the library foundation to support children's programming in 2000. This was done because the committee believed that children's programming had the necessary statistical information behind it to create a strong proposal. The committee also believed that children's programming would enhance the library foundation's ability to conduct fund-raising: People might be more likely to donate money to the foundation if they knew that it supported programming for children in the community. The committee's request for funding from the foundation (fig. 5.1) has many of the components essential to any proposal. It is concise. It clearly explains why the need for increased funding exists. It ties the request to the mission. It provides useful statistics. It includes relevant anecdotal data (patron comments). And the proposal explains how success will be measured, which ensures the foundation that the applicants realize that they are expected to spend the money wisely. ▃▃▃▃▃▃▃▃▃▃▃

FIGURE 5.1
Funding Proposal

MEMO

TO: Library Foundation

FROM: Children's Librarians Roundtable (CLRT)

DATE: 9/9/99

RE: Children's Programming 2000 Grant Request

CLRT would like to thank the Foundation for the continued support of children's programming at JCPL. Historically, a portion of the library's budget was dedicated to children's programming, with little or no money designated specifically for adult or young adult programming. Because of the Foundation's generous support of children's programming, the library has been able to increase the number and the quality of programs for the adult and YA audience. As adult and YA programming gains momentum at JCPL, the library is committing its resources to building and maintaining programs for this audience.

Since the library will be pursuing approximately $10,000.00 for adult and YA programs, CLRT is looking to the Foundation to supplement the programming budget, enabling children's programs to be fully funded in the upcoming year.

During 1999, CLRT coordinated 122 programs, attended by 5,340 children system-wide. Our programs ran the gamut and featured dynamic presentations from the Raptor Education Foundation, puppeteers, storytellers, artists and musicians. This summer, children were able to see live eagles and falcons, create treasures from recycled materials, experience a Madagascar cockroach and other insects up close, and be enchanted by storytellers, puppeteers and actors. These highly successful, interactive programs were presented for only 25 cents per child.

We are excited at the possibilities that exist for the Foundation and CLRT to work together in presenting quality programs to the communities we serve. We are confident that we can coordinate a dynamic schedule of programs for children and their families, with the Foundation's support. The attached grant request outlines our specific funding needs.

Jefferson County Library Foundation

GRANT APPLICATION FORM

Name: Children's Programming

Date: September 9, 1999   Library: JCPL   Department: Children's

AMOUNT REQUESTED: $17,600.00

☐ DESIGNATED FUNDS   ☐ UNDESIGNATED FUNDS   ☐ TECHNICAL ASSISTANCE

PURPOSE OF GRANT

Specify if the request addresses the needs of staff, library operations, patrons, other. If patron: what segment of the population is affected by the need; Documentation of needs.

The Library currently offers special children's programs for 7–8 months out of the year. Performers in the areas of arts, science and culture are engaged to present programs at each of the library branches. As the evaluations and statistics show, these programs are very popular and serve to establish the library as a focal point in the community for families. Parents and children look to the library to provide high-quality programs that extend the library's physical collection and mission.

The following table illustrates the types and costs of programs offered in 1999.

1999 CHILDREN'S PROGRAMS

Program	Month	# performances	Cost per performance	Total cost
Fun with Science	January	12	$127.50	$ 1,530.00
Jafrika	February	12	$125.00	$ 1,500.00
Oh the Animals	April	11	$150.00	$ 1,650.00
*Puppeteer, Bob Aiken	June/July	12	$185.00	$ 2,225.00
Merry Andrew Afoot	June/July	11	$ 70.00	$ 770.00
Creative Exchange	June/July	10	$ 87.50	$ 857.00
*Beetles, Bugs . . .	June/July	12	$ 75.00 + mileage	$ 1,170.00
John Orlando	June/July	11	$100.00	$ 1,100.00
Storyteller, Bett Kopit	June/July	11	$200.00	$ 2,200.00
Raptor Foundation	June/July	11	$ 50–$100.00	$ 1,160.00
Dave Sullivan	June/July	11	$ 65.00	$ 715.00
David Williams	June/July	11	$150.00	$ 1,650.00
Crystal Clown (bookfair performer)	August	5	$ 95.00 per hour	$ 1,485.00
Robert Hansen (bookfair performer)	August	2	$ 75.00	$ 150.00
Sugar & Spice (bookfair performer)	August	4 hours	$100.00 per hour	$ 400.00
Angel Vigil	October	9	$100.00	$ 900.00
WOW Outreach	November	10	$150.00	$ 1,350.00
			1999 Total	**$20,812.00**

*Please note, due to construction, the Wheat Ridge Library was not included in the following program schedule, with the exception of the asterisked programs.

To maintain the level of programming offered in 1999, the following budget is estimated.

(Continued)

FIGURE 5.1
Funding Proposal (Cont'd)

PROPOSED 2000 BUDGET

Estimation based on current schedule of special programs, with no additional performers

14 programs annually for 11 branches at average cost of $150 = $27,600

(includes 2 performances throughout year for CL and
2 performances in summer months for SL and BL)

ESTIMATED 2000 COST	$27,600
LIBRARY CONTRIBUTION (from branch book sale funds)	– $10,000
FOUNDATION REQUEST	$17,600

METHODS

Substantiate the strategy or activity which will be used to achieve the desired results. Why is this procedure the best course of action?

- The Children's Librarians Roundtable will research and select performers. The programming representative for CLRT will check references, negotiate prices, schedule and coordinate all performances.

- A Children's program featuring an outside performer will be scheduled for all branches for each month, with the exception of March, May, September, and December.

- A program per week will be scheduled for the 8 weeks of Summer Reading Club for all branches.

- Large branches, such as Columbine, Standley Lake and the new Belmar Library, will have two scheduled performances of each summer program to accommodate larger crowds.

EVALUATION

How will you evaluate the results?

The overall success of Children's Programming will be measured through participant evaluations and gathered statistics.

- Statistics covering the number of program attendees per branch are kept throughout the year and reported monthly to library administration.

- Program evaluations are distributed to participants and their parents during each program. Library staff compiles participant evaluations, completes a staff evaluation and submits all to the Programming Committee.

Department Head (for undesignated funds): _____

1999 Children's Program Coordinator

Foundation Director: _____

Friendly Programs

Although you might initially go to your Friends or foundation in search of a check for programming, in time you might want to encourage these groups to assist with the entire planning process. In chapter 2, we explored the workings of a program steering committee. We placed a library foundation member on this committee. By having a Friends or foundation member on the program steering committee, you have a person who understands how programs are produced. This person will see programming ideas at their inception and might see a program that he or she would like to cosponsor. This (it is hoped) means that the Friend or foundation member will partially or entirely fund the program in exchange for his or her name being included on any publicity the library creates. Ideally, you will have Friends who come to understand all aspects of programming, including contacting the performers and submitting the paperwork. This can be a great asset to your library, particularly if staffing is one of your budgeting constraints.

Let's assume that your Friends group has begun producing programs. The likely intent of this programming is to do one or more of the following: raise money, educate the community about library resources, educate the corporate or political community about the needs and resources of the library, and create goodwill and recognition for the library.[3] These programs could range from a free, Friends-sponsored authors series to promote National Library Week, to a $50-a-plate fund-raising dinner with a keynote address by a best-selling author. Some of these events might be held in the library, while others will be held in rented ballrooms. Even though all your patrons will not be able to afford the swank dinner-with-an-author, this program will generate money that can later be used for additional library programming. Be sure that your patrons understand that this is not a library-initiated program. Ask the Friends to clearly advertise the event as a Friends-sponsored fund-raiser, so that your patrons understand why this program is not free.

Do you have a library foundation (or Friends group) with 501(c)(3) tax-exempt status that contributes money to your programming efforts? If so, you should mention the foundation on your pro-gram flyers, on the programming link on your Web page, on the public service announcements on the radio, and anywhere else someone might read or hear it. When possible, include a line that mentions that the foundation is a 501(c)(3). People look for 501(c)(3) organizations when they want to donate money. People like to give money to organizations that have a good image. A library foundation will appeal to people.

Another recent, interesting development is the appearance of online databases where donors can give to the charities of their choice. These databases contain just about every 501(c)(3) that files with the Internal Revenue Service. An example of this type of Web site is allCharities.com. Investigate some of these Web sites. See if your library foundation is listed. Most of these sites give you 100 percent of the donation. If your library foundation is listed, then you might want to consider placing a link to the charities Web site on your programming Web page. Or the library foundation might want to add a link to its Web page. People really do use these sites. The Literacy Coalition of Jefferson County (Colo.) recently received a $75 donation via one of these sites.

Local Funds

Before we move on to landing the big fish—the grants—let's talk about what we can do in the local waters. Your library's financial situation and programming policy will guide your fund-raising efforts. For example, let's assume that your programming policy allows authors to sell their books after a reading. You could allow authors to bring their books to the program and sign and sell them afterward. Or, your Friends group or library foundation could purchase the books, and you, the program coordinator, could sell them to your patrons before the author signing. This would be convenient for both authors and patrons. Authors don't have to carry their books to the library; your patrons get a book signed. But do you sell the books at no profit to the library, or do you raise the price by a dollar or two and generate some money for your Friends or foundation? It could depend on the specificity of your programming policy.

Remember all the money the library spends on in-kind expenses for equipment, staff, and facilities? Other agencies and companies in your community can offer you in-kind support. Approach these groups with an offer that is mutually beneficial. They supply you with meeting space or food, and you publicize them as cosponsors. Don't beg. Make a proposal. It really is beneficial for a local grocery store to get its name on your program flyers. People like libraries, and people like companies that support libraries. A donation of snacks in exchange for printing the company's name on your flyers is a fair trade. It's probably a tax deduction to boot. See if you can establish a relationship with local theaters and hotels. A cosponsorship could result in a play being held in a beautiful auditorium or a dance workshop taking place in an elegant ballroom.

After you've gotten the hang of cosponsorship, it's time to approach local companies, individuals, and institutions to get them to fund an entire program series. This undertaking is more appropriate for your Friends group or foundation, if you have them. The preceding case study detailed the process by which a library received funding from its library foundation for a program series—the children's summer reading club. Now that the club has a proven track record, with statistics and good word of mouth, the next step is for the foundation to put together a presentation for potential funding sources. The presentation should include such information as the number of children who participate, which we know is over five thousand. The foundation could offer the funder a byline that reads "This Children's Summer Reading Club Is Made Possible through the Generous Support of Brett's Burgers." This is good public relations for Brett's Burgers. And Brett can write this off as a tax-deductible contribution. Everyone wins.

A final word on corporate sponsorship: Share the wealth. As we will discuss in chapter 8, local businesses must compete with one another to survive. Think of a way to make the sponsorship open to as many businesses as possible. If more than one business steps forward, have a plan in place. This plan could be as simple as placing the companies' names in a hat and drawing a winner. Perhaps you could also set a time limit for the

sponsorship. Invite new sponsors to compete for the honor every three years. If no one applies, keep the sponsor you have. Whatever your plan, be sure that your current sponsor understands the terms.

Grants

The Basics

In *Getting Your Grant,* Peggy Barber and Linda D. Crowe list what they call the Ten Commandments for Successful Grants. These commandments are:

1. Develop a project that enhances the goals and objectives of the library.
2. Involve the staff in every step—developing an idea, funding strategy, the proposal, and its implementation.
3. Be sure the library has the basic resources to support the project.
4. Thoroughly research potential funders.
5. Confirm the interest of a potential funder before writing your proposal.
6. Consider the funder a partner in the project, not a silent source of money.
7. Write a proposal that is clear and concise, demonstrating vision and technical competence.
8. Prepare a budget that is detailed, comprehensive, and realistic.
9. Be prepared to publicize the project when funded, during implementation, and when completed.
10. Build and maintain a relationship with the funding organization.[4]

The ten points listed above nicely encapsulate the grant-seeking process. The whole idea of writing a grant, however, can seem completely overwhelming. Until recently, I had never applied for a grant in my life, and I had no idea where to begin. In the fall of 1999, I attended the Colorado Association of Community Educators/ Colorado Adult Education Professional Association (CACE/CAEPA) Conference in Colorado Springs,

Colorado. Jenifer Federico of Denver Public Schools Community Schools Program presented one of the workshops I attended. The workshop was titled, simply, "Grant Writing." In an hour, Jenifer brought me from a fear of grants to an understanding of them.

Through Jenifer I learned that I must do a few things before I begin seeking support for my program. I must first make sure that my program has a direct link to my mission statement. My program should have measurable objectives. If I am seeking funding for an English as a Second Language program that teaches adults how to speak English, then I must develop a way to later measure whether the program has reached this goal. It is also helpful to form relationships with other agencies in my community, and then develop a program that does not duplicate an effort offered by another agency. Funding agencies are attracted to unique ideas. Ideally, my program will already be in place with a documented history of success. A program that has a proven track record is attractive to funders.

Funding sources include local and national foundations, government agencies, and corporations. Jenifer spoke about the importance of finding out all you can about the potential funder's mission. Funding sources frequently have very specific priorities. Sometimes they limit their funding to a geographic region. Take a look at which programs have recently received funding from this source. Does your program have anything in common with the programs that were funded? Also, take a look at the average amount of funding awarded by this source. Does it seem to offer much less or much, much more than you need?

Jenifer wrapped up her presentation by talking about the proposal. It is helpful to contact the funding source before you mail your proposal. Call on the telephone and introduce yourself and your program. You might want to mail information about your library and your program. Create a fact sheet. The American Library Association can help you. One of the pages on its Web site contains quotable facts you can integrate into a fact sheet. For example: Reference librarians in the nation's public and academic libraries answer more than seven million questions weekly. Standing single file, the line of questioners would stretch from Boston to San Francisco. Facts such as these are available at www.ala.org/pio/quotablefacts.html. A sample fact sheet on one of the branches of the Jefferson County (Colo.) Public Library is shown in figure 5.2.

After reading this information, the funder may very well call or write back and ask for a proposal. When it is time to submit the proposal, it is imperative to do what they ask of you. If the funder provides you with an application, fill it out completely. Many funders use a scoring system similar to the rating system libraries use when evaluating job applications. Do not give the funder a reason to lower your score because of an incomplete application. If you are unsure of what the application is asking, call the funder and ask. If the funder asks you to write a proposal from scratch, follow the guidelines if they are provided. Some funding sources will ask that your grant be submitted in a particular format. For example, funders in Massachusetts may ask applicants to use the AGM Common Grant format. This means that you would submit your grant in the format developed by the Associated Grantmakers of Massachusetts. (Examples of this form are located at www.agmconnect.org.) Be sure to ask for a specific amount of money, but also be sure that the amount you ask for is within the funding range. And don't forget the KISS principle—Keep It Simple, Stupid. Funders will not understand jargon and acronyms. So you'll want to elaborate on what you mean if you say that ALA recognized your library as offering one of the best ESL classes to YAs in the state.

Finally, if your proposal is turned down, call the funding source and ask what you can do better next time. Many funders will be happy to help you better prepare for the next round of applications.

Resources for Finding Grants

As you begin to look for funding sources, some standard titles will help you immensely. The *Annual Register of Grant Support: A Directory of Funding Sources* and the *Foundation Directory* are both excellent.[5] Your state probably has a directory as well. For example, Colorado has the *Colorado Grants Guide* and *Mickle's Directory of Colorado Foundations*.[6] The Foundation Center's

FIGURE 5.2
Library Fact Sheet

A SHORT

H · I · S · T · O · R · Y
GOLDEN LIBRARY

The Golden Library, the oldest library in Jefferson County, was incorporated on February 7, 1914, after a year of planning by four local women's organizations: the Bay View, Fortnightly, Progressive, and Thursday Musicale. Members of the four organizations incorporated as the "Golden Library and Improvement Association." The group bought property at 713 13th Street, improved the existing building with the help of the men and boys of Golden and opened the Library. The library remained at that site for 49 years.

The Jefferson County Commissioners authorized the formation of a county library in 1952. In 1961 the Golden Public Library merged with the Jefferson County Public Library, and in so doing, set a standard of cooperation between city and county which continues to the present.

In May, 1961, both the Golden Library and the Jefferson County Public Library administration moved into the "new" Golden Civic Center at 911 10th Street, using quarters donated by the city. Those quarters now house the Golden Police Department.

In 1966, in another example of city-county cooperation, a site next to the city hall was set aside by the city for county use as a building site for a new Golden Library. The library moved into its new building in June of 1970, and the Jefferson County Public Library administration moved to temporary quarters in the Applewood Grove shopping center. The move to the modern building, designed by local architects William Coppock and Robert Dunham, marked the first time the Golden Library was housed in a facility specifically designed for library use.

In the mid 1990's, when it became apparent that the library was outgrowing its quarters, the city and county once again worked cooperatively to rehouse the library. The result was a trade between the city and county, with the county receiving the former recreation center, and the city receiving the library building located at 923 10th St.

The "new" Golden Library, opened on May 4, 1996, is twice the size of the 1970 library, and many times the size of the original 1914 structure. Architect David Anderson of Andrews and Anderson, has designed a totally renovated structure which combines the flexibility and functionality of a modern library with traditional Golden themes. The new building is designed to provide up-to-the-minute library service to the growing Golden area population.

by Ada Jo Barber

Building Features
•Building was gutted and renovated to be flexible, to accommodate changing needs and technologies well into the future.

Statistics
•Staff 13 salaried employees, 6 shelvers. Total 19
•Collection
Access to the shared collection of the Jefferson County Public Library's 800,000 books. Also offers high tech information resources.
•Library Size Approximately 14,000 sq. ft.
•Cost of Renovation and Furnishing $1.8 million

Architect	*Andrews and Anderson*
Contractor	*Centerre Construction*
Interior Design	*Unter Design*
Project Manager	*ACR Engineering*
Funding	*The People of Jefferson County*

Special thanks to the Board of County Commissioners for a one-time funding grant, to the Golden City Government and the Citizens of Golden for making the building swap possible and to GABLES for tireless pursuit of a darned good idea.

Golden Library
1019 Tenth Street • Golden, CO 80401
(303) 279-4585

Monday - Thursday	10:00 a.m. - 9:00 p.m.
Friday & Saturday	10:00 a.m. - 5:00 p.m.
Sunday	Noon - 5:00 p.m.

Jefferson County Public Library

Web site has many links that will help you find funding sources. Their Web site address is fdncenter.org. The professional literature will frequently carry the RFPs (requests for proposals) of funding sources. Your state library newsletter is also a good source for announcements of grant opportunities for libraries.

It is a good idea to become familiar with the National Endowment for the Humanities (NEH), your state humanities councils, and the American Library Association (ALA). The NEH funds many library projects, such as "Choices for the 21st Century." The Choices series is a scholar-led reading and discussion program that engages citizens in discussion about selected public policy issues, such as immigration and the environment. The NEH's Web site is www.neh.fed.us. ALA receives funding from several sources, including the NEH, for traveling exhibitions, discussion programs, literary programs, and other library cultural programs for adults. Many of these programs are scholar-led, such as "From Rosie to Roosevelt: A Film History of Americans in World War II." This program uses documentary films, readings, and discussions to involve library audiences in studying the American experience in World War II. Information on these programs can be found on ALA's Web site at www.ala.org/publicprograms.

You will also want to look into the Library Services and Technology Act (LSTA). Your state library administers the funds. The funding is intended for two broad priorities. The first is activities that use technology for information sharing between libraries and other community services. The second is programs that make library resources more accessible to urban, rural, or low-income residents, and others who have difficulty using library services. Each state has a five-year plan outlining its programs. These programs support the LSTA goals, which are to:

- establish or enhance electronic linkages among or between libraries;
- link libraries electronically with educational, social, or information services;
- help libraries access information through electronic networks;
- encourage libraries in different areas and different types of libraries to establish consortia and share resources;
- pay costs for libraries to acquire or share computer systems and telecommunications technologies; and
- target library and information services to persons who have difficulty using a library and to underserved urban and rural communities.[7]

Although much of the money awarded via LSTA grants goes to support the use of technology in libraries, many libraries receive money to do creative programming. For example, in 1998 the Escondido (Calif.) Public Library received an LSTA grant to support on-site literacy programs and basic library services for families housed in a women's shelter. The grant also provided funding for a parental reading and educational curriculum, and trained adult literacy tutors who worked with ethnically diverse learners. Another successful LSTA-funded program occurred in Connecticut. The Prosser Public Library focused its energies on increasing the services and materials available to its African-American patrons. The library celebrated Black History Month in February 1998 with a two-part, scholar-led discussion on the Amistad incident. Over fifty people attended the discussions, many of whom had never been to the library. This program was supported by increasing, markedly, the African-American collection in the library. The new materials proved very popular—with a circulation rate four times above that of the general collection. Average monthly circulation for the entire library increased sharply—nearly 50 percent.[8]

The Grant Proposal

We've already discussed the importance of contacting the funding source ahead of time. Now that you are ready to submit your proposal, be sure you've involved those people who will need to sign off on the grant application before you submit it. This may be your director or library board chairperson. A grant may provide the funding that allows you to greatly expand or enhance your programming. With the help of a state department of education grant, you might now be able to offer literacy tutoring to adults three days a week. This is a wonderful thing. Just be sure that your administration and library board have had the chance to discuss the project with you along the way. People feel much less threatened by innovation if they've seen it coming and are prepared for it.

As for the proposal itself, you will either have an application to fill out or you will submit your own proposal. Ask the funding source if you can see examples of successful applications or proposals. There is an excellent chance that they will show you examples. (Many of these sources are publicly funded and the applications they receive become public record.) There are many excellent sources on proposal writing, such as *Proposal Planning and Writing.*[9] The Foundation Center's Web site (fdncenter.org) contains a proposal writing course that provides the following proposal outline:

Executive Summary: umbrella statement of your case and summary of the entire proposal (1 page)

Statement of Need: why this project is necessary (2 pages)

Project Description: nuts and bolts of how the project will be implemented (3 pages)

Budget: financial description of the project plus explanatory notes (1 page)

Organization Information: history and governing structure of the nonprofit; its primary activities, audiences, and services (1 page)

Conclusion: summary of the proposal's main points (2 paragraphs)[10]

After you've written and submitted your proposal, your work really begins. In the event that you are not funded, you should get in touch with the funder and find out what you can do to receive funding next time you apply. But let's expect success. When you are funded, write a thank-you letter to your funder. Describe how you plan to publicize the program, crediting the funder as a sponsor. Send copies of the flyers and other publicity. If a funder has picked up a major, ongoing event, such as an adult summer reading club, ask if the funder would like to become a member of that event's steering committee. The more you involve your funders and give them a chance to see your programs in action, the more dedicated they will become. Also, be sure you are clear on the evaluation and reporting process. Begin collecting whatever data you will need, including quotes from the people who have attended and appreciated the program. Show your funder the "Thank You's" from your patrons.

Now that we have generated some money, let's move on to the fun part: finding something to spend it on!

Endnotes

1. Debra Wilcox Johnson, *Cultural Programs for Adults in Public Libraries: A Survey Report* (Chicago: American Library Association, 1999), iv.

2. Ibid., iv–v.

3. Sandy Dolnick, ed., *Friends of Libraries Sourcebook,* 3rd ed. (Chicago: American Library Association, 1996), 153.

4. Peggy Barber and Linda D. Crowe, *Getting Your Grant: A How-to-Do-It Manual for Librarians* (New York: Neal-Schuman, 1993), 2.

5. *Annual Register of Grant Support* (New Providence, N.J.: R. R. Bowker, published annually); and *Foundation Directory* (New York: Foundation Center, published annually).

6. *Colorado Grants Guide* (Denver: Community Resource Center, published biannually); and *Mickle's Directory of Colorado Foundations and Government Grants* (Littleton, Colo.: Mickle, 1997).

7. Institute of Museum and Library Services, *Grants to State Library Agencies* (Washington, D.C.: The Institute, 1999), http://www.imls.gov/grants/library/lib_gsla.asp.

8. Ibid.

9. Lynn E. Miner, Jeremy T. Miner, and Jerry Griffith, *Proposal Planning and Writing,* 2nd ed. (Phoenix: Oryx, 1998).

10. The Foundation Center, *A Proposal Writing Short Course* (New York: The Center, 1995–2000), http://fdncenter.org/learn/shortcourse/prop1.html.

6
Selecting a Topic

THIS IS THE FUN PART! WHO DOESN'T LIKE TO COME up with a bright idea? The computer books have been circulating well . . . let's try a program on buying a home PC. The stock market has been up and down lately . . . let's ask an economics professor to come in and give a talk on the history of the New York Stock Exchange. A patron suggests that you hold a singles mixer at the library on Tuesday evenings. All these ideas might translate into successful library programs. But *first* you must ask yourself if these programs tie into your library's mission. The first two ideas mentioned above seem to qualify as instructional programs. The likely purpose of the third program is to welcome people into your facility. You may want to draw potential new patrons into your building, or you may consider it part of your library's mission to be a community gathering place. Your mission will help you determine your topic.

Your ideas can be influenced by the source of your funding or resources. If your library foundation pays the performers' fees for most or all of your programs, then your foundation may very well request or expect quite a bit of input with programming topics. Ideally, the library foundation will be integrated into your program commit-

tee (see chapter 2); this will allow the foundation to contribute equally in the planning process. Another fairly common situation is for programming to be turned over partially or entirely to a library's Friends group. This is usually done because (1) program planning—from thinking up an idea, through the performance itself and the evaluation—can take a great deal of staff time, and Friends groups can take on many of these programming responsibilities; and (2) programming can be a lot of fun, and this can be a powerful recruitment tool when your Friends group wants to increase its membership. If you tell people that they can help plan and produce concerts and plays and other cool things if they join your Friends group, then some people *will* join and eagerly work on developing programs. Again, it is a good idea to get someone from the Friends group on a program committee. This cooperation and collaboration is vital. Library staff need to remain partners in the process, because they will most likely be the people who, at the very least, create the publicity, arrange for the necessary equipment (such as projectors and screens), and reserve the meeting space. Library staff are also the folks who will be asked for details on upcoming programs. Therefore, staff need to be kept informed of forthcoming programs and the performers, even if library staff were not the ones who planned and funded the programs.

Now, let's proceed with choosing a topic.

What Are the Joneses Doing?

What are other libraries doing? A recent study titled *Cultural Programs for Adults in Public Libraries* received usable responses from 1,229 medium- and large-sized libraries serving populations of five thousand and more.[1] The survey asked libraries to give participation rates for nine program types. The results are shown in the following list:

Book discussions	61.4%
Author readings/presentations	59.3%
Lecture series	43.8%
Musical performances	41.7%
Dramatic performances	22.9%
Adult reading incentive programs	20.1%
Film series	19.8%
Creative writing workshops	18.2%
Dance performances	14.2%

Let the Collection Be Your Guide

Which of the program types listed in the preceding table interest your library users? You most likely know the answer. You know what questions patrons are asking at the information desk. You know which items are always checked out, on hold, or being ordered and reordered. Books on buying computers, herbal medicines, and cooking always seem to be in demand. Perhaps a faculty member from a local college could give a sixty-minute presentation on things to look for (specifications, price ranges, and name brands) when buying that first home computer. Or, perhaps a local chef belongs to an association such as the International Association of Culinary Professionals. If the holidays are approaching, a program on healthy holiday cooking might be popular. Monitoring your collection won't tell you what your community as a whole is interested in (some people just don't visit the library), but it will show you the areas of interest to your library patrons.

Get All Staff Members Involved

Library staff work with your patrons throughout the day. They very likely also live in the community. It's important to let all staff know that they are welcome and encouraged to generate programming ideas. Circulation staff, for example, see firsthand which materials are circulating. The discussions that take place at the circulation desk are frequently more informal than elsewhere in the library. Patrons, while checking their books out, will talk about what they are reading, what they are doing later in the day, what they like about the library. Patrons will also tell the circulation staff about things they don't like, or they'll suggest additional materials and services. Speaking with the circulation staff provides an accurate snapshot of what your patrons are reading, viewing, listening to, and requesting.

Library patrons often approach an information desk and ask, "I saw something about X on the news the other night. Do you have anything on that?" Or, "I was listening to NPR this morning, and they did this whole piece on that singer, X." The staff working your information desks will know what current event topics are of interest to your patrons.

In order for these ideas to come from staff, it's important to empower staff in the creative process. Your library may have a programming committee that arranges programs, or programming may be done at a branch level. However it's done, it is a good idea to let your *entire* staff know that they are encouraged to submit ideas. When staff get excited about programming, they will become an endless source of creative ideas. And, you will find that members of your staff possess some previously unknown talents. Suddenly a colleague will be volunteering to lead a workshop on quilting or baseball card collecting. Or a staff member will come to you with the names of friends in the community who have skills and hobbies that they are willing to share with other library patrons.

Tie Programs into Holidays, Festivals, and Celebrations

When planning programs, especially over the course of a year, you may want to look at what holidays and celebrations occur during the year. For example, a library may want to schedule a program in May to tie into Cinco de Mayo. *Chase's Calendar of Events* is a great resource to use when brainstorming programs.[2] Let's say you want to plan a program in September, but you just can't think of a topic. If you open *Chase's* to the September section, you will find that September, among other things, is Baby Safety Month. Perhaps you could ask someone from a local organization or association (such as the National Association of Parents) to give a talk on selecting a baby-safe stroller and car seat. *Chase's* is also a good tool to use when you have an idea but are unsure of when to schedule the program. For example, you've decided to produce a program on basic bicycle repair and maintenance, you've located a speaker, but you're just not sure when to have the program. When you check under "bicycle" in *Chase's* index, you see that May is National Bike Month.

Other Sources of Inspiration

Your state library most likely also has information that can help you tie into local and national events. The State Library of Colorado, for example, sends to libraries throughout the state a packet of information on National Library Week. The packet includes program ideas, outreach activities for elected officials, sample press releases, and clip art for promotional flyers. Check to see if your state library offers similar materials.

Local newspapers are also a good source of ideas. Scan the events sections of your local newspapers. You might want to plan programs that will complement an upcoming traveling exhibit at a nearby museum. The classifieds are also a good section to browse. Pay close attention to people who are advertising their services. If someone is advertising her services as a masseuse, perhaps she would be willing to offer a lecture and demonstration at your library in exchange for

being allowed to hand out her business cards after the program.

Of course, you'd like to hear directly from your intended audience if possible. How do you solicit library patrons and your community for ideas? Community input could be gathered through a survey (see chapter 4), the formation of an advisory board, or a suggestion box in the library. Realistically, however, your library's resources may not permit you to develop, distribute, and tabulate the results of a survey. Do you have the staff time needed to form and serve on an advisory group? If the number of staff hours you are able to dedicate to programming is limited, the best way to generate community input may be through your evaluation process. (Sample evaluation forms can be found in chapter 12.) Be sure that your evaluation forms contain a section that asks participants what programs they would like to see in the future. It doesn't hurt to ask this question directly to the audience as you are collecting the evaluation forms. Ask, "What other types of programs would you like to see the library offer?" Programming is a grassroots process. If you are just beginning to offer programming in your library, it may take a while for the audiences to grow in number. But as they do, the participants will become more and more enthusiastic, and you will begin to receive evaluations with such comments as, "Great! Thanks so much for offering this. How about something on writing a will?"

When thinking of potential programs, ask yourself what agencies and groups exist in your community. Would your local genealogy society send someone to speak on how to start a family tree? Most communities have local offices of such associations as the American Heart Association or the American Association of Retired Persons. The local chapters of these associations will most likely have speakers with prepackaged workshops and lectures. You would not need to do much more than offer them the use of your facilities and produce some advertising.

Pop or Classical?

Chances are that your library's mission statement will give you quite a bit of flexibility in determining which topics you choose. A silent film series or a lecture on Alzheimer's are probably both within bounds. You will probably create a programming calendar that mixes the recreational with the informational. The two really do blur anyway. Often, learning begins when you discover a topic that gives you pleasure. I know a great deal about movies because I first began watching them as a toddler with my grandfather. I then began attending them as a kid on my own, went on to read books about the history of movies, and ended up studying film as an undergraduate in college.

Some programs you will offer because you know the library is a good venue for dispensing the information—the *classical* programs. You might ask representatives from local agencies to give talks on arthritis, pest control, living trusts, and a variety of other topics. Just as you know that this information should be found in your library in book format, you believe this information should also be available to patrons in the format of a program. Other programs will aim simply to please—the pop. You'll aim for the Martha Stewart– and John Grisham–type programs—the best-sellers. It's great fun planning programs that you know will draw large crowds. Your "how to" programs, such as how to buy a computer or how to cook a feast in thirty minutes, can really bring 'em in the doors.

From a program planning standpoint, you will want to estimate your audience turnout when you select your topic. For example, if you decide to offer a microwave cooking workshop,

ask yourself how many people will attend the program. Just take a guess. How many people will attend a program on applying for a home loan? You will want to ask these questions early on. If you foresee that the program will be heavily attended, you might want to ensure that your publicity mentions that tickets will be required. If you decide that the program may not draw a large crowd, it doesn't mean that you shouldn't offer the program. It just means that you will have to be more diligent with your publicity. You might have to call some local agencies and organizations and talk up your program. You might have to spend some extra time identifying businesses that might be willing to post your flyer. If you can reach the people who need the information, they will come to your program. For more on publicity techniques, please see chapter 10.

Sometimes a program will form around a desire to meet the needs of a particular group of people. Your idea for a program on arthritis, for example, could originate from an attempt to offer a program for your senior population. The following chapter details how you can begin offering programs geared toward a target audience.

Endnotes

1. Debra Wilcox Johnson, *Cultural Programs for Adults in Public Libraries: A Survey Report* (Chicago: American Library Association, 1999), iii.

2. *Chase's Calendar of Events* (Chicago: Contemporary Books, published annually).

7
Your Target Audience

ALL PROGRAMS BEGIN WITH AN IDEA. THERE ARE AT least three variations of "the idea." First variation: Someone has a topic in mind, such as baseball card collecting, and begins planning a program around that topic. The preceding chapter covered ways in which you can select and pursue a topic. Second variation: Some staff person or group decides to target a particular audience type. For example, your library decides to begin a series of summer programs that you hope will draw more young adults into the library. One of the programs in the series will feature a magician and another will present an airbrush artist who will help teens create their own T-shirts. Third variation: You know of a talented performer in the community and you approach him to present a program at your library. This third scenario will be covered in the following chapter. In this chapter, we will focus on scenario two: the target audience.

Target audiences will certainly come up at the beginning of the year if you divide your programming budget into categories, such as adult, YA, and children. If you outline your programming goals at the beginning of the year (as discussed in chapter 2), then you will probably also discuss intended audiences at the same time. This really just amounts to you planning a variety of pro-grams to meet the demands of your entire community. You'll want to include women, men, the young and the elderly, business owners and self-employed artists, the exercise fanatics and those with health concerns. You'll select various topics that you hope will appeal to many of these people. One person might fall within many of these categories. A fit, elderly, businesswoman might show up to your program on stroke prevention.

Your programs are, of course, open to everyone, but it can be an exciting challenge to try to offer a program with a particular audience in mind. Perhaps you have noticed, when running around doing errands during lunch, that Latinos work at many of the local shops and restaurants. You never notice Latinos in the library. Would a particular type of program bring them in? It might, but what topic would you choose? If you have some knowledge of the Latino population in your neighborhood, then you might be able to select a topic that will appeal to them. If you need a little help, just remember that organizations exist to help you. Such associations as REFORMA (National Association to Promote Library and Information Services to the Spanish Speaking) should have local chapters that can offer insight into the interests and needs of your

Latino community. Your library collection will have resources that list associations at the state and local levels.

Expanding Your Horizons

When we begin to pursue programming for Latinos, teenagers, our deaf patrons, and others, we sometimes learn that we are not very knowledgeable about the people we want to serve. This doesn't mean that they are that different from the fitness buff or the single mother; they may *be* the fitness buff and the single mom. But you may still face some challenges. For example, if you want to offer a job-hunting workshop in Spanish, but no one on staff speaks Spanish, then you have a challenge ahead of you. Acknowledging a challenge does not make you politically incorrect or insensitive. Sure, Spanish speakers are a diverse group who cannot be typified. They will have many of the same interests as your English-speaking patrons. They will enjoy sports, appreciate good cooking, and have concerns about their retirement, and your Spanish-speaking patrons will attend your library's programs on these topics if they feel comfortable doing so. But let's assume that some of these patrons have approached you and, in a mix of Spanish and English, they've told you that they prefer programs in Spanish. You pursue this with library administration and they say that it sounds like a fine idea. The thing is, no one on staff speaks Spanish. What do you do?

You will be tempted to "just do it." You've already done your demographic work, and you know that the Spanish-speaking community exists. Why not just offer some programs? Ask yourself: If I "just do it," will I be offering a quality program? If you attract a large number of Spanish speakers into your library for a program, and afterward they walk out onto the floor to ask reference questions, borrow books, and get a library card, will you be able to serve them? If yes, then go for it. If the answer is no, you may want to pursue this audience in a more strategic fashion. To continue using a Spanish-speaking audience as an example, let me present a case study that illustrates how one library began offering services to this group.

The Jefferson County Public Library (JCPL) is located just west of Denver, Colorado. (If you haven't guessed it already, I'll 'fess up: I work for JCPL.) Part of the county stretches into the foothills of the Rocky Mountains. Once an agricultural and mining area, Jefferson County now is a thriving suburban, business, industrial, and residential community with a population of nearly five-hundred thousand. The library consists of seven full-service branches open sixty-three hours a week. The library also has five extension branches whose hours range from six to forty-three hours a week. One of the libraries, the Villa Library, was located just a mile west of the city of Denver. (The library has since been relocated to a new facility and renamed.) In the spring of 1997, I was the head of reference and adult services at the Villa Library. We began noticing that people whose first language seemed to be Spanish staffed many of the small businesses and restaurants surrounding the library. The library's administration, justifiably, wanted something a bit more concrete than anecdotal evidence gathered through staff visits to the mall. In order to get the entire Villa Library staff involved in this learning process, we invited a representative from the Latin American Research and Service Agency (LARASA) to our staff meeting. The representative explained some of the characteristics of the Latino community in Jefferson County. (LARASA is a nonprofit organization created in 1964 to improve the health, education, and self-sufficiency of Colorado's Latino community.) We learned about the population trends, the incomes, occupations, countries of origin, languages, families, and income levels of the Latino people in the Villa area. The importance of the extended family was discussed. We learned that if we wanted to attract Latino children to the library, we should tap into the mothers. And one of the best ways to tap into the mothers was to go to them and let them know that they were welcome in the library. But where do we find the mothers? we asked. Make an appearance at their churches, the LARASA representative told us.

After the LARASA presentation, we began to put together a demographic report from data collected from such sources as the school district, the census, and local organizations. The study, completed in April 1998, revealed that approximately 9 percent of the people (11,506 residents) in the Villa service area were Latinos. The study also detailed such characteristics as countries of origin, education, and income level. Through the study we learned that the majority of Latinos in Colorado (60 percent) report that English is their primary language, while 30 percent report Spanish as their primary language, and 30 percent report that they are bilingual. This meant that almost thirty-five hundred people in the Villa service area spoke only Spanish.

After viewing the demographic study, library administration gave the go-ahead to begin exploring ways in which the library could serve its Spanish-speaking residents. At this point, although library staff—myself included—were itching to begin buying books and offering other services, the library paused and took a breath. The library decided to lay some groundwork before offering resources and services specifically targeted toward Spanish-speaking Latinos. The pause occurred because the library was not adequately prepared to serve its Latino population. Staff members were not prepared, the collection was not in place, and no paperwork, such as library card applications, existed in Spanish. Where should we begin? We decided that it was time to offer the staff some additional communication skills.

Communication really is a two-way street. All people communicate better when they are in a comfortable situation. In order for library staff to communicate well with patrons, staff must comprehend the patrons' needs and then provide them with the answers or resources they seek. The Villa Library staff just needed the necessary training to make this communication possible. With this training, we would feel more confident and open in our interactions with Latino patrons—particularly those who spoke Spanish. And the Spanish-speaking patrons would feel less awkward when asking for assistance if they knew that we were knowledgeable about their language and culture.

At this point it might not hurt to repeat that I am not suggesting that a great deal of training needs to occur in order for you to communicate with someone who fits under a demographic heading of "Hispanic" or "Over 65." Everyone is an individual, whether that person is Hispanic, over sixty-five, male, female, single, divorced, etc. But, if one of these groups seems to not be using your library, there may be a reason. By learning more about that group and the attributes its members share in common, you can put yourself in a better position to serve them.

In the summer of 1998, the Villa Library hired an instructor to offer basic Spanish classes to the staff. Ninety-minute sessions were held once a week for six weeks. The staff attended on library time. This six-week basic language series was followed by another six-week series focused more on library-related words and phrases. We learned how to tell a patron, in Spanish, that his book is due in three weeks. We also learned other library standards, such as "The library's phone directories for the United States are on CD-ROM" and "Do you know how to use the microfilm/microfiche machine?" All staff members were given a cheat sheet of these phrases in English and Spanish.

With the classes under way, some of the Villa staff made a trip to a distributor of Spanish-language materials and purchased a small number of adult, YA, and children's books. The library also added a few magazines in Spanish and added Spanish to our directional signs within the library so that patrons would become aware of our intent to offer materials and services in Spanish. We also drafted a new section for our collection development policy dealing with the collection of Spanish materials. By this time, staff were excited about the opportunity to offer these new materials and services. In the beginning, the only service we could offer was a few slowly pronounced phrases in Spanish, but the benefits were immediately noticeable. Instead of mutual panic breaking out when a non-English-speaking patron approached an only-English-speaking staff member, both parties relaxed when they realized that between the two of them, they spoke just enough English and Spanish to help one another understand the question and the answer. Instead of being intimidated by the language differences, staff members looked forward to the challenge.

After making sure that staff were included in and comfortable with the process, we began concentrating on ways to promote the materials and resources to the Latino community. The Villa Library experimented with a Spanish story hour. We offered tours to English as a Second Language (ESL) classes. We translated our library card application and welcome brochure into Spanish. We began working with local organizations to help us identify the wants and needs of the Latinos in our service area, and we made appearances at the meetings of organizations that served Latinos, such as REFORMA, and promoted our services and materials. We submitted job postings to newspapers and electronic mailing lists aimed at the Latino communities, and now have a staff member on board who is fluent in Spanish. A Spanish/English article recently appeared in our library newsletter. We visited other libraries, such as Denver Public Library, that had been offering these services for quite some time, to learn from them. So, where are we now with programming for Latinos? Well, we are gaining ground all the time. We have offered a Spanish/English storytime. We have offered programs that focused on Latino culture. For example, we invited a *santero* (a person who carves saints) to give a demonstration on *santos,* which are carved and painted saints' figures. And even though we have yet to offer a program entirely in Spanish, we now have the staff and resources in place to do so. We have also learned more about our Latino patrons. We have learned that most of them have someone in their family who speaks English. This opens up the possibilities of targeting some programs toward our Latino patrons, yet offering the programs in English. Ideally, the flyers and other publicity would be in both Spanish and English. Musical programs are a good choice for audiences of mixed languages. There is usually little talking done by the performers. Latinos frequently attend programs as a family, and one of the members usually speaks enough English to help the others along. We have also learned that you can ask a staff person who speaks Spanish, perhaps a library page, to walk among the crowd and help those people who do not understand what is being said. Because we have patrons who prefer to hear their programs in Spanish, we will offer some programs entirely in Spanish. We have laid a lot of groundwork. We are now ready to move on down the road. ▬▬▬

Putting Your Experience to Work

Once you have learned how to expand your traditional programming into other areas, you will find that the same process can be used again and again. What if, after you have begun offering programs in Spanish, you decide to begin offering intergenerational programming? Many of the steps mentioned in the preceding case study can be applied to intergenerational programming. In her excellent book entitled *Intergenerational Programming,* Rhea Joyce Rubin notes, "Intergenerational programs combine people of more than one age group in a mutually beneficial, mutually enjoyable activity."[1] An intergenerational program involves more than gathering the young and the elderly in the same room together. A stamp-collecting workshop that happens to attract both children and seniors is not an intergenerational program. An intergenerational program is a planned event. An entire chapter of *Intergenerational Programming* is dedicated to the importance of planning and preparation. A planned intergenerational program might bring children into contact with a group of seniors who are experienced stamp collectors. The program becomes truly intergenerational when the two groups begin to interact, when the children begin to ask questions about the stamps and the relevance that they have to the collectors' lives.

Children and seniors do have some unique characteristics. For example, seniors are used to being able to make their own decisions, while children are used to being told what to do but appreciate the opportunity to make choices themselves. Identify the agencies in your community that serve seniors, such as the Retired Senior Volunteer Program (RSVP). These agencies can contribute information, supply or recommend senior volunteers who have worked with children, and promote your program to their clients. But before you begin offering intergenerational programs, make sure that the staff have the necessary training. Just as some of your staff might not be prepared to effectively help Spanish-speaking patrons, some of your staff will need to learn more about a particular age range. Some training is probably in order to prepare your staff to work effectively with an audience that could range in age from six to eighty-six. For some intergenerational programming ideas, try ALA's Office for Literacy and Outreach Services Web site at www.ala.org/olos/intergenerational.html. In addition, ALA's *Whole Person Catalog* (www.ala.org/publicprograms) includes a section on discussion programs for special audiences.[2]

Becoming More Inclusive

As you become expert at offering programs for particular audiences, you will acquire the skills that will enable you to make all your programs more inclusive. Once you have learned how to modify your services and collections to respond to community needs, you can produce programs that will be attended by all members of your community. Often, your programs will target a particular portion of your population. But many of your programs will target a general audience. You will offer a program on a particular topic, such as travel in Europe, and you will hope that anyone who is interested will attend. Ideally, you will provide the environment that makes this possible. For example, we've seen how bilingual publicity and the presence of a bilingual volunteer can make our Spanish-speaking patrons feel welcome at a library program, even if that program is in English.

The way in which you present your programs is very important. Do you structure your programs in a way that makes them accessible to most or all of the members of your community? For example, do you give deaf patrons the opportunity to request an interpreter? Are your performers informed when an interpreter will be present? A more inclusive program might take additional planning and time. The performer might need to meet before the program with the deaf patron and the interpreter to work out the seating arrangements. You will be surprised at how easily you can integrate everyone into your programs by making a few room modifications and by providing the necessary adaptive technology (such as an assistive listening device for an audience member who is hard of hearing).

A good program will attract an audience, and that audience might include a Spanish-speaking person, a deaf patron, a person with a learning disability, or all three. All these people will have more in common than they have differences. Yet we will want our library to meet everyone's needs both during and after the program. We will want materials relating to the program that are useful for everyone. We will want staff who are able to help the patrons find the materials. We will want facilities that accommodate everyone. This involves planning. Gerald Jahoda and William L. Needham's *Improving Library Service to Physically Disabled Persons* includes checklists that libraries can use to determine how well their facilities, resources, and staff (in terms of training) meet the needs of physically disabled patrons.[3] Included in the appendixes is an article Jahoda wrote in 1980 entitled "Suggested Goals for Public Library Service to Physically Disabled Persons." The following portion of the article gives insight into the planning that is involved when you begin to expand the accessibility of your library services.

> Goals for public library service to visually, hearing, or mobility handicapped persons are discussed in terms of material, equipment, facilities, services, staffing, including use of volunteers, liaison with organizations of and for handicapped persons, involvement of handicapped persons in the planning and evaluation of library services, publicity, and funding.[4]

Other excellent resources exist that will help you learn how to offer inclusive programs. For example, in 1999, the American Library Association published *Guidelines for Library Services for People with Mental Retardation.* These guidelines state the following:

> People with mental retardation use the library for the same purposes as other library users. Their interests are generally similar to the interests of their age-mates. They come to the library seeking information, recreation, instruc-

tion, and inspiration. They can become enthusiastic, effective, responsible library users. Many are fond of books and computers and enjoy storytelling, read-alouds, movies, magazines, and music. Their abilities are usually less recognized than their disabilities, but they have both. Their disabilities require modifications of services and collections as well as of the facility itself if they are to be full participants in the library's programs. Modifications should build on their abilities and strengths.[5]

The guidelines go on to state:

> Library programs are adapted for the enjoyment and pleasure of people with mental retardation, including adapted communication and the use of multiple formats. When planning programs and other activities, library staff members build in opportunities for people with mental retardation to interact with each other and with people who are not mentally retarded. Opportunities are provided for learning and practicing social skills. Appropriate interactions are modeled for both individuals with mental retardation and other library patrons.[6]

When you have learned how to adapt your services and collections to include all members of your community, then you have truly made your library accessible to a general audience.

Outreach

In this chapter, we have explored how you can identify a particular, potential audience, such as seniors, and develop programs, collections, and services to meet that audience's wants and needs. We have also looked at ways that you can make all your programs accessible to all your patrons through planning and through the modification of some of your services and resources. Now that you have this knowledge, we can investigate the possibility of extending your services beyond the library's walls. Let's talk about outreach.

Let me quote from yet another source. In *Managing Library Outreach Programs,* Marcia Trotta says:

American society is undergoing rapid, sweeping changes. In order to meet the changing and growing needs of our communities, it is becoming a *basic service* to reach out beyond our walls and make library services not only *accessible,* but also *relevant* to diverse populations. Library services must be shaped not just by our professional perceptions but by "customer-focused" planning. This means service that goes beyond the traditional realm of what we have offered in the past, and far beyond the clientele to whom we have offered it.[7]

Outreach has become a basic service for many library systems. Some libraries have a Coordinator of Outreach Services and some even have an Office of Outreach Services. Other libraries must squeeze an outreach program in here and there as staff and time allow. Regardless of the number of staff you can dedicate to outreach, all libraries begin by asking, "Why should we offer outreach programs?" and "To whom are we going to offer this service?" A common answer to "why" is that it brings your services to the people who want and need them. The answer to "who" narrows the scope of the potential audience. Everyone in your community does not visit your library. Some don't come in because they can't, some stay away because they may think your library has nothing for them, and others stay away because they just aren't interested. The first two groups are the people who are most likely to respond to outreach. If the residents of a nursing home can't visit the library, you can bring a program to them. If the Russian-speaking people in your neighborhood don't see how the library relates to them, you can ask to speak at their church and announce the materials and services you have for them. Outreach is always a great public relations vehicle.

If the local businesspeople in your neighborhood are too busy to visit the library, you can ask to visit them at a chamber of commerce breakfast and give a presentation on the business resources available at the library. Outreach shows the library's goodwill, and some of the people you make the effort to visit will begin visiting you in return.

If you have done some outreach in the past, you know that it's almost impossible to do alone. You will want to form partnerships. Although you are reaching out to many people, these people usually congregate in a place. Many of the seniors in need of outreach will be in senior centers or nursing homes. A local church might offer a weekly service in Russian. The demographic work you did back in chapter 4 should help you identify the appropriate church or senior center. These agencies very well may call *you* and ask you to pay them a visit. On the other hand, your demographic work might have told you that certain groups of people just aren't using your library. So you decide to go to them.

This will be the only time you will read these words in this book: It's okay to *not* have a plan at this point. When you get the senior center or church representative on the telephone, introduce yourself and ask if you can pay a visit to some of their members. Bring an assortment of relevant library materials, bibliographies, and library card registration forms to the meeting. Introduce yourself, and describe any materials or resources that you think will catch their interest. If you have books in Russian, or if you have staff who speak Russian, let your audience know. If you have any services that will make the library more convenient for them, mention it. For example, does your library deliver books to agencies? New immigrants who are intimidated by the idea of visiting your library might get a library card if they knew they could pick up and return their books at their church. Better yet, can the church staff and the library work out a way to set up a small, satellite library in the church? Be sure you use part of your time at the meeting to ask questions and listen. Ask them what services would get them to visit the library. And ask them what services they would like to see offered at their church or senior center or other neighborhood location. Would they attend a parenting class? an English as a Second Language class? a financial aid workshop? Would the class need to be in Russian? After you have ideas, work with the staff of the hosting agency (the church, community center, etc.) to make the program a reality.

As Marcia Trotta indicated, the programs will have to be relevant to the participants. Ask them to participate in the planning process. The seniors at the senior center might tell you that they want a book discussion group, but they might not like the title you choose. Let them choose. Use the staff of the hosting agency as a resource. Ask them questions. Your program will alter shapes many times before it becomes a reality. For example, when I worked for the New York Public Library, I volunteered to co-lead a book discussion group with another librarian at a senior center on Staten Island. At first we decided to offer a monthly book discussion group. The staff at the senior center told us they thought that some of the participants might have trouble finishing a book in a month. So we decided to have a short-story discussion. We picked a short story, mailed it to the center for distribution, and asked the senior center staff to have the participants read the story ahead of time. Then we showed up for the discussion. Some people hadn't read the story because they couldn't read the type. Those who had read it enjoyed the discussion. Those who hadn't been able to read it asked a lot of questions, such as "I don't know what the hell you are talking about. Who died in the end? I couldn't read the story. What happened?" We learned our lesson.

The next month we sent another story, but this time we enlarged the type on our photocopier first. However, at the next discussion we learned that one lady still couldn't read the story because she was legally blind. After thinking about this challenge for a while, one of us had the bright idea to read only stories that were available on Talking Books from the Library of Congress. We got the lady a machine that played the Talking Books and trained the senior center staff on how to use it. We then picked a story that was both in the library's print collection and on a Talking Book. We ordered the Talking Book, photocopied an enlarged paper copy, and mailed both to the center ahead of time. Once again we showed up for the discussion. Some people still hadn't read the story, but, this time, it was by choice. They asked a lot of "What happened?"–type questions, but the other participants responded to them by saying things like, "Betty, you have to read the story to know what happened." It was amazing how direct the group could be with one another. Learning how the group communicated—being able to tell when they were angry or just engaged—took time and patience. The group also adapted to us. We began to choose stories that we knew both the participants and the group facilitators—my partner and I—would enjoy. We had created a program that was accessible and relevant to everyone.

The possibilities with outreach programming are almost endless. Frequently, libraries offer a certain program topic or program format both in-house and off-site. You have seen how a book discussion, which many libraries offer in-house, can be modified and offered as an outreach program. A topic such as preparing for United States citizenship might be popular both within a library branch and at a nonlibrary location, such as a family learning center. For example, the Boulder (Colo.) Public Library is a member of a community organization called the Boulder County Immigration Advocacy Coalition. The coalition presents programs, such as informational meetings with a volunteer immigration lawyer, in the library and at locations throughout the community. Please see chapter 4 of Trotta's *Managing Library Outreach Programs* for some detailed examples of outreach programs that might work for you.[8]

As you begin to plan your outreach programs, be sure to set more time aside than you would for your average library program. There is probably a reason why you are bringing a program to a group, instead of the group coming to you. In its current format, your in-house program might not be useful to your target audience. You might have to modify your program in some way. You have seen how a book discussion became a short-story discussion with some additional modifications that allowed everyone to "read" the story. Modifications take time. You may have to collaborate with someone who speaks Spanish in order for you to bring a computer instruction class to a community center. And, finally, because you are sending staff in cars, subways, buses, or taxis to other locations, you will have to consider commute time when creating your schedules.

In chapter 6, you explored various ways in which you can select a topic. In this chapter, you learned how to gear programs toward particular audiences, and how to modify your library services and materials in order to make them more inclusive to all members of your community. You have done a lot of preparation. Now you can have some fun, and perhaps spend some money. It's time to go out and find some performers who can make your ideas a reality!

Endnotes

1. Rhea Joyce Rubin, *Intergenerational Programming: A How-to-Do-It Manual for Librarians* (New York: Neal-Schuman, 1993), 3.

2. *The Whole Person Catalog No. 4: The Librarian's Source for Information about Cultural Programming for Adults* (Chicago: American Library Association, Public Programs Office, [1999]).

3. William L. Needham and Gerald Jahoda, *Improving Library Service to Physically Disabled Persons* (Littleton, Colo.: Libraries Unlimited, 1983).

4. Gerald Jahoda, "Suggested Goals for Public Library Service to Physically Disabled Persons," *RQ* 20 (winter 1980), quoted in Needham and Jahoda, *Improving Library Service,* 109.

5. Standards Committee Subcommittee to Develop Guidelines for Library Services for People with Mental Retardation, *Guidelines for Library Services for People with Mental Retardation* (Chicago: Association of Specialized and Cooperative Library Agencies, American Library Association, 1999), 8.

6. Ibid., 12–13.

7. Marcia Trotta, *Managing Library Outreach Programs: A How-to-Do-It Manual for Librarians* (New York: Neal-Schuman, 1993), vii.

8. Ibid., 43.

8
Identifying the Right Performer

As I was writing this chapter, I knew that I would also write a chapter called "Choosing the Best Format." I immediately realized I had a what-came-first-the-chicken-or-the-egg scenario on my hands. Do you need to know what format your program will follow before you begin looking for performers, or do you first find out if there is someone in your community who has expertise in the topic before you spend a great deal of time fretting over the format? I decided that quite a bit of give-and-take occurs between the program coordinator and the performer. You might call the performer with a great idea for a lecture on the history of jazz. The performer, however, might explain to you that she finds it much more effective to perform certain jazz songs on her trumpet and then give a brief talk on the history of the song afterward. In reality you will need to have a fairly clear idea of what format you are looking for, because the performer will very likely ask you what topic you would like presented and how. The solution to the which-chapter-to-read-first conundrum might be to set aside an hour and read this and the following chapter as companion pieces.

At last: You are ready to bring a performer into the library! This is fun stuff. You have ideas and you have permission to get someone to come into your library and *do* something. Let's see: You've heard a lot of people asking questions about computers at the information desk . . . so, how about a program on buying a home computer? Your uncle knows a lot about computers, but so does the guy at the corner computer store, and you had this great teacher a couple of years ago when you took a continuing education class. . . .

Who gets the job? A useful trick might be to think of programming as another aspect of collection development. What would you do if you were looking for a computer book? You would be interested in content, you'd probably want a book from a reputable publisher, and you wouldn't want to spend a fortune. If your programming policy doesn't get into the details of hiring a performer, take a look at your collection development policy. Here's what a typical collection development policy (this one from the Jefferson County [Colo.] Public Library) says about selecting materials:

> Factors that librarians consider when deciding which materials to purchase include:
>
> - interests of library users
> - level of material
> - accuracy of presentation

- uniqueness of viewpoint
- timeliness or permanent value of content
- author's reputation or credibility as authority
- publisher's reputation
- price
- durability, appropriateness of binding and format

Most of these qualities—interest to library users, accuracy of presentation, price, etc.—would be applicable to performers. "Level of material" could pertain to the intended age level of the audience. Perhaps "durability" and "binding" aren't so relevant, unless your performer is a mummy!

Now that you are more comfortable with the qualities you are looking for in a performer, it's time to begin the search.

Staff Members as Performers

When you are seeking a performer, it will occur to you to look for staff members who can present or perform programs. Be careful here. Let's say that you have identified a need for a job-hunting program. You don't have anyone on staff who is an expert on this topic, but you supervise a librarian who has excellent presentation skills, so you approach her and ask her to develop a ninety-minute job-hunting program. She carefully studies the topic and creates a PowerPoint presentation and a bibliography. It takes her eleven hours over the course of three weeks to put this together. She presents the program and the audience evaluation forms are unanimously positive. Is the program a success?

If patron education classes are within the mission of your library, then the answer most likely is yes. Such a program can be wheeled out again and again when the need arises. This program can also be shared with other libraries. But how many of these staff-produced programs can your library create? They are certainly costly in terms of staffing. If you intend to offer more than one program a month, you will probably want to turn to local community members, agencies, and associations for potential speakers. The missions of many local and national organizations include

community outreach. Frequently these groups (American Association of Retired Persons, Consumer Credit Counseling Service, etc.) will send someone to your library at no cost; rarely will you pay more than $50. The material and presentation skills that these groups offer are usually excellent.

Let me elaborate a bit here. Library staff are excellent presenters of information. Libraries all across the country and world have librarians presenting programs on genealogy, Web-based shopping, basic computer skills, and a myriad of other important topics that are in high demand. But many of the libraries that use their staff as presenters have trained these people to do so. This can be an elaborate process. First, some or all of your staff are trained in the learning patterns of your target audiences—adults, children, young adults, or other populations. Then this cadre of staff learn how to develop the format and content of a program. This involves learning when to use overheads versus flip charts, and how to break up a program or class with hands-on activities. The staff apply these skills they've learned by creating programs. Ideally, these programs (how to search the Internet, how to conduct genealogy research on the Web, etc.) are previewed in front of a test audience before they go live. When a program is ready for the public, the staff members who developed the program then train their peers in how to present it themselves. The class can then be taught at a variety of times and locations by several staff members. In the end, you have two wonderful resources. You have a collection of terrific programs that can be scheduled at any time with minimal preparation, and you have a collection of staff who now have the skills to develop quality programs and classes on any topic imaginable. But it takes time to get there. Such books as *Teaching the New Library: A How-to-Do-It Manual for Planning and Designing Instructional Programs* and *Teaching the Internet to Library Staff and Users* will help you get there.[1]

The other scenario that you will encounter involves identifying a staff member with expertise in an area that sounds perfect for programming. Your head of circulation is an accomplished rock climber. One of your pages is an investment whiz. What do you do? Some of your patrons might be more likely to attend the program if a staff person whom they know presents it. The program will undoubtedly be well produced and well received. Are there any cons? Well, again, it comes down to staffing. How much time was spent preparing for the program? Will that person be compensated for this preparation? Could someone from the community have been brought in at less expense? And last, and this might sound harsh, would your patrons be better served if you brought someone in from a local or national organization? We, as librarians, usually seek to purchase materials from nationally recognized publishers. Should we do the same with our performers? Ideally, your staff member will be affiliated with an organization. Perhaps the rock-climbing staff person is also a member of the Mountaineers. Adding a speaker's affiliation to the publicity can give more authority to the program and, therefore, increase your attendance.

Performers from Local Businesses

The programming policy and procedures you've developed will help determine which performers you seek. Public libraries that receive all or most of their money from residents' tax dollars might want to be careful about hiring performers who own their own business or work for a business. In fact, there may be laws that address whether your city or county can use tax dollars to promote individual businesses. This means that if you hire someone from Zack's House of Birds to give a talk on birds, you might have to ask Zack to refrain from mentioning his business during his talk. And you will want to make sure you don't give the House of Birds a mention on your flyers or in your newsletter.

Even if no laws are in place, another bird store owner may become annoyed if she feels that you are giving Zack the spotlight by asking him to speak. Why didn't you also ask Kim of Kim's Cockatiels to speak? This does happen. Competing businesses will not be pleased with your library if they feel you are producing an infomercial on a competitor's business. If you do seek someone from a local business, you'll want to have a policy in place that states to what extent he or she can mention the business. Some libraries ask performers to limit the mention of their business to an introductory sentence. "Hello. I'm Zack and I have a Ph.D. in animal husbandry and in 1972 I opened Zack's House of Birds on 13th Street and 1st Avenue." You might also allow the performer to place a stack of business cards on the table before or after the lecture.

Hiring a local business owner has benefits. These people work with birds or cars or computers every day, and they are going to be very knowledgeable and extremely enthusiastic. But there are things to watch for. Your local mechanic, for example, might not perform at many speaking engagements. Be sure to ask what experience she or he has with public speaking. And, the mechanic may be very tempted to mention to the audience that if indeed someone's car is acting up, she or he can have a look at it and give a free estimate. I had a program go completely off the tracks once when a stockbroker from a specific brokerage firm, who was supposed to be giving a brief nuts-and-bolts explanation of investment strategies, began telling patrons ways in which he could make them heaps of money if only they'd use him as their broker. To avoid this worst-case scenario, set the boundaries before the performance, and, if possible, attend the performance yourself to see how the material is covered.

When you contract with a performer who owns or works for a profit-making business, ask if he or she belongs to a society or association. Zack may belong to the American Birding Association. If so, you can ask him to use that as his primary source of authority when giving his lecture. Instead of saying, "As the owner of Zack's for the last twenty-eight years . . .," he should talk about his relationship with the association. You can also include this information on the flyer. This is probably consistent with your policies in other areas, such as your bulletin board. While you would likely post a flyer from the nonprofit American Birding Association without hesitation, you would most likely not post a flyer announcing a 50-percent-off sale at Zack's.

In reality, business owners, stockbrokers, and others will present many of your programs. They know that libraries are good publicity mechanisms. These people are extremely knowledgeable and most of them are fine speakers. If you establish parameters well before the program, you'll be fine. But remember to set the parameters: Ask speakers to limit the mention of their business to an opening introduction, and remind them that they can place a pile of their business cards on the table. Check over their handouts, and ask them to tone down or remove letterheads and other materials that promote their business or attempt to recruit clients. There are times when you will want to find someone from a local business to present a topic. These people are experts; if they weren't, they wouldn't be in business. If someone is going to speak to your patrons about computer repair, it's a good idea to hire a professional.

If a local business approaches you and asks to present a program in your library, you might discuss the content of the program and decide to produce it. But, if you decide that the program is not appropriate for library sponsorship, you still might feel that people in the community are interested in the topic. If this is the case, and if you have a meeting room in your library, then you could remind the business owner that he or she may rent (if there is a fee) the room and present the program. The program then becomes an event sponsored by the business, not by your library. The business would be responsible for creating the publicity and handling whatever registration might be involved. This approach can also be used when organizations, such as the American Heart Association, ask if you would like to sponsor an informational program on heart disease. Because these organizations usually have a comprehensive publicity system in place, it might be appropriate for you to donate the meeting space and let the organization handle the publicity and other logistics.

Other Performers

Now that we have thoroughly explored the pros and cons of using a local business owner, it's time to get back to locating a performer. The topic of the program will influence where you look for the performer. A professor who has a great deal of experience in studying and possibly treating depression could present a quality program on depression. Therefore, you're likely to look for someone with an academic background. A local college's speakers' bureau might be a good place to start. If you are looking for a musician to play some jazz during a grand opening of a new library, you probably want one who plays well; you won't be too concerned with educational background. The newspaper's music section might give you a lead in locating a local instrumentalist or jazz band.

Finding Performers

If you decide to seek performers outside your library staff, you'll be relieved and amazed to discover the places you can turn to for assistance. Here are some strategies you might want to use when seeking performers:

Call the universities and colleges in your area. Funding for many schools is contingent upon their offering services, such as volunteer work, to their communities. Ask them if they have a speakers' bureau or a catalog of faculty members willing to speak to community groups. A surprising number of colleges have detailed catalogs listing subjects and faculty members who speak on these subjects. The schools will usually mail these catalogs to you. Ninety-nine percent of the time, these professors will speak for free.

Use print resources, such as the *Encyclopedia of Associations*.[2] For example, if you know you want to sponsor a program on heart disease prevention, you can check under "Heart Disease" in the index. One of the associations listed is the American Heart Association. You can then call the national number, or you can check your local telephone directory to see if there is a local chapter. Many national associations have a number of ready-made lectures and workshops that they can present, most likely at no direct cost to your library.

When looking for artistic performers, such as musicians or actors, local newspapers are a great resource. Check the "Community" or "Arts" section of the paper. Who is performing? If you see a program that coincides with what you are seeking, give the performers a call and see if they are able to perform in your library. Also, check the sections in the classifieds that allow people to advertise their services. You'll find such sections as "Musician's Services" and "Musicians Wanted/Available." If you're looking for someone to play classical guitar in your library, see if someone is offering acoustic guitar lessons in the classifieds. Call and ask if she or he would like to perform in your library.

Call or contact other libraries and ask if they keep a list or database of performers. Ask them to share this information with you. If you have access to the Internet or e-mail, join regional and state electronic discussion lists concerned with library-related issues. This is a quick way to ask hundreds, perhaps thousands, of people at once for help. If you are working via the telephone or post, the *American Library Directory* is a good, standard source for library addresses and phone numbers.[3] Your state library is also a good resource for programming ideas, publicity ideas, and potential performers. And while you are investigating at the state level, check the Library of Congress's Center for the Book at lcweb.loc.gov/loc/cfbook/stacen. html. Your state might have a Center for the Book affiliate that is dedicated to promoting or sponsoring literary events and projects.

You really will be surprised at the number of organizations in your community that will offer performers at little or no cost. And, once you begin offering programs fairly frequently, people and organizations will catch word of this and they will begin calling *you.* Figure 8.1 lists some of the performers who appeared in the Jefferson County Public Library in 1999.

FIGURE 8.1
Examples of Program Performers

AGENCY THAT SUPPLIED PERFORMER	TITLE OF PROGRAM	PROGRAM DESCRIPTION	COST
Colorado Student Loan Program	College Financial Aid Planning	Provided financial aid tips for parents and teens	Free
Colorado State University	Barn Again! Preserving Colorado's Agricultural Heritage	Talked about historic barns in Colorado and the efforts to preserve them	Free
Colorado Division of Wildlife	Wildlife Watch	Provided information on the Colorado Division of Wildlife's program that trains people in wildlife appreciation; offered tips on watching animals in the wild	Free
Rocky Mountain Quilt Museum	Quilts!	Talked about the history of quilts, collecting quilts, and how to care for quilts	$50 per location

National Traveling Exhibits and Initiatives

There is yet another option open to you when seeking a performer. Once you have identified a topic that you would like to pursue, the next step is to seek a performer. Usually you begin looking for someone from your community. You also might want to contact your state library or state humanities council to see if they are funding or producing any traveling exhibits or initiatives. For example, the "Choices for the 21st Century" discussion series is an initiative that is currently being produced in many libraries around the United States. This discussion series of international issues was developed at Brown University. In Colorado, the initiative is being produced by the National Endowment for the Humanities (NEH) and the Colorado Endowment for the Humanities. A scholar is provided to the library at no cost. The library hosts four discussion series covering such topics as immigration, China, and the environment. The library purchases the materials for the participants ($100 for twenty-five booklets). The library does have some paperwork to fill out and submit after the series concludes. This might be an ideal program to pursue if you are seeking someone to lead a current events–type program at your library. Information on this initiative is available at www.choices.edu.

The American Library Association (ALA) produces many programs funded by such agencies as the NEH. Check ALA's Web site at www.ala.org/publicprograms. Here you will find information on how your library can host a scholar-led discussion series, such as "From Rosie to Roosevelt: A Film History of Americans in World War II." The "Live at the Library!" project gives libraries grant opportunities to present nationally known authors. The ALA Web site also provides information on how your library can host traveling exhibits, such as "The Jazz Age in Paris," a portable panel exhibition. Your library will probably be asked to pay a fee for these exhibits, which may or may not cover the shipping costs. Fees usually begin at around $600 for a six- to eight-week exhibit. These exhibits and projects do require a commitment of staff time that involves filling out applications and other paper-

work. But they offer your library the chance to sponsor beautifully produced programs and exhibits that your patrons will surely appreciate, hopefully in large numbers. For more information on traveling exhibitions and national and state programs, be sure to get a copy of the *Whole Person Catalog* at www.ala.org/publicprograms.[4]

Contacting Performers

Once you've chosen a topic, selected a format for the program, and identified a potential performer, you're ready to give the performer a telephone call. Chapter 2 discussed guidelines and procedures that are helpful to have in place before you begin programming. It's assumed then that you've checked calendars and budgets and whatever else first. Before you call, however, it's a good idea to have a checklist in front of you. This checklist will guide you in asking the performer the right questions, such as "How much will you charge to perform?" and "What days and times are you available?" The checklist in figure 8.2 can be used when negotiating with a performer on the telephone.

The days and times that a program is held can be very important. The makeup of your community will help you determine when to schedule programs. Is your library located within a bedroom community? If so, you might want to plan programs for later in the evening, because people will need time to commute home. Some seniors will ask that you hold programs in the afternoon, because they cannot see well at night, or because they eat dinner early and go to bed shortly thereafter. Teenagers might be willing to pop into the library on the way home from school, but homework and other activities might keep them from returning to the library later in the evening. If you live somewhere that offers great events and weather on the weekends, can your library event compete with other community events and the great outdoors? It is a good idea to have a target audience in mind when scheduling a performer. If the program is going to be held at other nearby libraries, you might want to vary the days and times and compare results afterward.

FIGURE 8.2
Program Performer Checklist

Name of Program: _____

Name of Presenter: _____

Telephone: _____

Before you call, fill out this section as the program coordinator:

KNOW WHAT YOU WANT FROM THE PERFORMER.

Topic of Program: _____

Length of the Program: _____

Format of the Program: _____

Meeting Space Available: _____

Month(s), days, and time of day you have in mind for program: _____

_____

Other: _____

_____

When calling the performer:

1. Explain your expectations.   _____

2. Get the days and times the performer is available within your time frame.   _____

3. Ask what the performer feels is fair compensation (have a ballpark amount
   in mind; i.e., $75–$125 per hour).   _____

4. Ask if the performer is willing to present at other branches.   _____

5. What is the performer's preferred audience? Adults? Children?
   Young adults? All ages?   _____

6. Let the performer know if he or she will need to use any assistive technology,
   such as the microphone from a voice amplifier. Will a sign language interpreter
   be present?   _____

7. Ask the performer to send you a brief biographical sketch (via fax or USPS).
   (This will help you determine the authority of the performer. It also provides
   your public information office with the information necessary to generate
   publicity.)   _____

8. Ask the performer to send you the names, addresses, and phone numbers
   of locations where he or she has appeared recently. Let the performer know
   that you may call these locations as references.   _____

9. Ask the performer to send (via fax or USPS) a brief outline of the proposed
   program. (This will ensure that you both agree on the content of the program.
   It also provides your public information office with the information necessary
   to generate publicity.)   _____

You and the performer should be specific and in agreement when choosing the program's length, because you will most likely need to book or set aside a meeting room for the event. It's also nice to either print the length of the program on the flyer or agenda, or announce the length of the program when you introduce the performer. People like to know how long they will be sitting. Ask the performer how much time she feels is needed to cover or perform the material. The format of the program (see chapter 9) will greatly influence the length. People can easily go two hours when involved in a group discussion; most people begin to squirm when a lecture goes beyond an hour.

After this initial contact with the performer, you will proceed with whatever process you have in place. (An example of the workings of a pro-gramming committee is discussed in chapter 2.) Most likely you will submit paperwork (see chapter 2 for examples) to some person or department. The performer should then receive a written confirmation. A standard contract can be developed for this purpose and can be used even if the performer is not charging for his services. This contract may be mailed from your library's business office. If you work for a small library system, or if your programming is done at the branch level, then you may be the person who writes this letter. A sample cover letter for a performer's contract and the contract itself are included in figures 8.3 and 8.4. The person coordinating the program should sign the cover letter. The contract should contain a list of all branches, and the dates and times of all performances should be listed next to the participating branches.

FIGURE 8.3
Sample Cover Letter for Performers

Date

Dear

Thank you for agreeing to present _____ at _____ branches of the Jefferson County Public Library.

CONTRACT
Enclosed are two copies of a contract for your presentations. The contracts have been signed by the Library Director. Please review the agreement, then sign and return one copy to me so I can submit a request for payment to the business office.

Jefferson County writes checks each Thursday. Please return your contract promptly in order that your check can be ready for you _____ .

SPECIAL ARRANGEMENTS
In order to ensure the best situation possible for your presentation, please let me know how you'd like the room arranged, how you'd like to be introduced, and whether you'll need any special audiovisual or presentation equipment.

DIRECTIONS
Please take a moment to look over the enclosed map of library locations. Let me know if you need more detailed directions.

If you have any questions, please do not hesitate to call me.

Cordially,

Name
Program Coordinator
Phone

FIGURE 8.4
Sample Performer Contract

CONTRACT

THIS CONTRACT is made _____ by and between the Board of Trustees of the Jefferson County Public Library (hereafter referred to as Sponsor) and _____ (hereafter referred to as Speaker) in connection with an engagement sponsored by Jefferson County Public Library, upon the following terms and conditions:

Arvada Library	Evergreen Library	Villa Library
8555 W. 57th Ave.	5000 Highway 73	455 S. Pierce St.
Arvada, CO 80002	(at Buffalo Park Road)	Lakewood, CO 80226
phone (303) 424-5527	Evergreen, CO 80439	phone (303) 936-7407
	phone (303) 674-0780	
Columbine Library		Standley Lake Library
7706 W. Bowles Ave.	Golden Library	8485 Kipling Street
Littleton, CO 80123	1019 Tenth St.	Arvada, CO 80005
phone (303) 932-2690	Golden, CO 80401	phone (303) 456-0806
	phone (303) 279-4585	
Conifer Library		Wheat Ridge Library
Conifer High School	Lakewood Library	5475 W. 32nd Ave.
10441 Highway 73	10200 W. 20th Ave.	Wheat Ridge, CO 80212
Conifer, CO 80433	Lakewood, CO 80215	phone (303) 232-4417
phone (303) 982-5310	phone (303) 232-9507	

TYPE OF ENGAGEMENT: _____

COMPENSATION:_____

TERMS OF PAYMENT: Payment in full after last presentation at the _____ on _____

ADDITIONAL TERMS: None

1. In the event that the engagement covered by this contract shall be prevented by weather, an act of God, physical disability, or any other cause beyond the control of the parties, Speaker and the Sponsor shall respectively be relieved of their obligations stated in this contract.

2. The Sponsor reserves the right to cancel this engagement for any reason at any time prior to 30 days preceding the engagement, voiding this contract and excusing the Sponsor from any payment or other compensation. If this contract is cancelled by the Speaker less than 30 days prior to the scheduled engagement, the Speaker will reimburse the Sponsor the amount of $_____ to help defray the production, promotion and labor costs that are incurred up to the date of the cancellation.

3. The Speaker shall indemnify and hold the Sponsor harmless from any claims or damages which arise from the Speaker's negligent or intentional acts or omissions.

4. No member of the Sponsor or of County government shall benefit from this contract. Violation of this clause shall cause this contract to be void and of no further force and effect.

5. The Sponsor reserves the right to audio or video tape record any lecture, reading or speaking engagement. The Sponsor may retain the tape in its files, may re-play the tape for its employees, and may make the tape available to Sponsor's customers. Sponsor shall make no more than three copies of the tape. Sponsor shall not sell the tape. The Sponsor shall provide a copy of the tape to the Speaker, upon the Speaker's request.

6. In the event expense reimbursement is included as compensation, the Speaker shall provide the Sponsor with receipts or similar documentation adequate to confirm the expenses incurred.

(Continued)

FIGURE 8.4
Sample Performer Contract (Cont'd)

7. The laws of the State of Colorado shall be applied in the execution, interpretation and enforcement of this contract, and venue shall be in the District Court in and for the County of Jefferson, State of Colorado.

8. This Contract is a personal services contract, and is not assignable by either party absent the prior consent of the other party.

9. This Contract represents the entire agreement of the parties hereto, and may not be amended except in writing signed by the parties.

SPONSOR:
BOARD OF TRUSTEES OF JEFFERSON COUNTY
PUBLIC LIBRARY

By _____

Library Director
Jefferson County Public Library
10200 W. 20th Avenue
Lakewood, CO 80215

SPEAKER:

_____
Signature

_____
Mailing Address

_____
Date

In addition to mailing the performer a contract, it is a good idea to contact the performer at least two other times before the program. If flyers are to be created for the program, you will want to mail a copy to the performer. You might want to offer a quantity of the flyers to the performer to distribute to friends, coworkers, and association co-members.

The final contact you make with the performer will be a confirmation call a week or so before the program to verify the dates and times. Ask if the performer has the directions to the library. Ask again about any equipment needs. Again ask if the performer will be distributing handouts. Will the performer reproduce these or will the library need to make copies from the originals?

This brings us right up to show time. Now let's backtrack. At the beginning of this chapter we realized that finding a performer and selecting a format (film series, film lecture, filmmaking workshop, etc.) occur almost simultaneously. The following chapter explores the various formats available to you as you plan your program. Let's find the format that fits your particular program.

Endnotes

1. Cheryl LaGuardia and others, *Teaching the New Library: A How-to-Do-It Manual for Planning and Designing Instructional Programs* (New York: Neal-Schuman, 1996); and William D. Hollands, *Teaching the Internet to Library Staff and Users: 10 Ready-to-Go Workshops That Work* (New York: Neal-Schuman, 1999).

2. *Encyclopedia of Associations: Regional, State, and Local Organizations* (Detroit, Mich.: Gale, published annually).

3. *American Library Directory* (New York: R. R. Bowker, published annually).

4. *The Whole Person Catalog No. 4: The Librarian's Source for Information about Cultural Programming for Adults* (Chicago: American Library Association, Public Programs Office, [1999])

9
Choosing the Best Format

IF YOU ARE READING THIS BOOK FROM FRONT TO BACK, this chapter might seem out of place. Shouldn't you know what format you want your program to take *before* you go out and find a performer? Well, perhaps. Certainly if you want to conduct a book discussion group, you have this format in mind when you begin your search for a discussion leader. When looking for a jazz band, you probably have a live performance in mind. At other times you might know that you want to present information on a topic, such as buying a laptop computer. Yet you are open to whichever format is most effective in conveying the information to your patrons. After you've found your computer expert to present the program, you consult with her on the best way to present the topic. She might suggest either a sixty-minute lecture or a two-hour workshop. After some discussion, the two of you decide that, with a workshop, she has more opportunity to interact with the patrons. She could bring a few examples of laptops to the program and allow the patrons to spend some hands-on time determining which computers they like best.

What Are Your Choices?

Which format is best for your program? Some of your programs will blend two or more formats. A classical guitarist might preface the performance of each piece with a brief story (lecture) about the origin of the song. Other format choices will be straightforward, such as your book discussion group. Let's attempt to put names to our choices in formats. There seem to be (at least) seven programming formats that recur frequently: speakers (lectures) and panel discussions, instructional presentations, workshops, demonstrations, live performances, discussion groups, and film or video series. I will define these formats, list some of their strengths and weaknesses, and give some tips that will help you when producing a program in a particular format.

Speakers and Panel Discussions

DEFINITION

Speakers tend to be experts on a topic. They usually arrive, speak on a topic, answer some questions from the audience, and leave. Panel discussions usually consist of several speakers seated behind a table. They each speak in turn, answer some questions from the audience, and then leave. Panel discussions are sometimes facilitated by a moderator who poses certain questions to the panel.

PROS

The speaker format is an excellent venue for an author or someone giving a personal account. For example, a Holocaust survivor's personal story would probably be presented in this format. Panel discussion can also be a very powerful medium. Fairly controversial topics can be addressed, such as immigration or the environment. Experts with differing points of view can express their beliefs and question the beliefs of the other panel members. Patrons can leave these discussions with a new perspective on a topic. Since speakers and panels frequently work without a script, you can ask them to tailor their discussions to your audience's particular interests.

CONS

The speaker/lecture format offers little audience participation. If your lecturer doesn't have strong speaking skills, your audience is going to lose interest quickly. Panel discussions take a great deal of time to organize. You must select all the speakers on the panel, and then you must make sure that each person understands her or his role on the panel. You might have to find a moderator as well to keep the program on track.

TIPS

Begin planning a panel discussion several months in advance. Because at least one member of the panel will end up canceling, have alternates in mind. Provide everyone involved with a list of the panel participants (including the performers' names, telephone numbers, and e-mail addresses), so that you and the participants can work out the details of the program's content. Send the participants an outline of the discussion that breaks the sections down into time periods. This will help keep them on schedule during the program. Try to have a staff person sit in the front row during the program and act as a timekeeper.

She can hold up a "1 more minute" sign when appropriate, so that the speakers know when to move on to the next section. Last, remember that people's attention span is shorter when they are not actively engaged. Your lecture or discussion panel should probably not go for more than an hour—ninety minutes if questions are taken at the end.

Instructional Presentations

DEFINITION

Instructional presentations are similar to the speaker/lecture format. In fact, presentations essentially are dynamic lectures. The goal of a presentation, particularly in libraries, is usually to instruct the audience on how to do something. Presentations frequently incorporate handouts, overhead transparencies or PowerPoint slides, practice exercises, and limited interaction with the audience. An example of a program in this format is a college financial aid presentation. The presenter might speak about specific scholarships and grants. She could then display an overhead transparency of a financial aid form. She might end the program with a practice exercise. She could distribute some books on financial aid to the audience and ask them to identify scholarships that seem tailored to them or their children.

PROS

A presentation is an excellent way to convey a great deal of information in a short period of time. People love this type of program when you hit on the right topic. A "job-hunting on the Internet" presentation might attract a large audience, especially if the participants can have access to the Internet during the presentation. If library staff conduct the presentation, the library will have copies of the agenda, an outline of the presentation's content, and handouts. This means that the presentation can be reproduced fairly quickly and easily by staff the next time around.

CONS

Because these programs take a great deal of preparation—creating transparencies, agendas, outlines, and exercises—they can be very staff-intensive when produced by library personnel. Try to bring in outside presenters if possible. Sometimes, someone in the audience will know either much more or much less than the rest of the audience; this person might comment afterward that the program was either too advanced or too simplistic. Use such comments as the basis for developing another program at a different skill level. Perhaps a patron comment regarding the simplicity of "Finding a Job on the Internet" will encourage you to pursue a future program called "Marketing Your Resumé on the Internet." Last, presentations can overwhelm people with information. People will then comment, "Too much stuff covered in too little time." Create an agenda that has three or four objectives. Less *is* more . . . or at least less is enough.

TIPS

You will want the audience to receive an agenda. This allows patrons to see what will be covered and bail out at the beginning if it isn't what they had in mind. If time allows, ask each audience member to tell the presenter why she or he is attending the program. This gives the presenter the opportunity to slightly alter the presentation in order to meet the expectations of as many patrons as possible. Remember that many adults learn through practice and examples. Don't just say, "There's millions of jobs on the Internet." Show them how to use a specific Internet site to find a particular job, and then, if possible, let them find a job that is relevant to them.

Workshops

DEFINITION

If instructional presentations are dynamic lectures, then workshops are dynamic instructional presentations. Workshops will contain the same elements as presentations: the handouts, slides or transparencies, the lecture component, and the exercises. The additional element is the "work." There will be many more hands-on opportunities. In a fiction-writing workshop, participants will get an opportunity to write something. In a Windows 2000 workshop, the participants will have opportunities to practice what they are learning. Workshops are usually at least two or three hours in length. In the case of a fiction-writing workshop, the program might be best offered as a three-part series. This will ensure that everyone has a chance to write a piece and have it critiqued by the instructor and other participants.

PROS

Workshops allow participants to learn by creating something. Even computer workshops on Excel or PowerPoint tend to have participants create their own spreadsheets or slide presentations. It's amazing to see people go into a workshop with reservations about their skills and come out with pride in what they've accomplished.

CONS

The same potential "cons" listed for instructional presentations also apply to workshops. It is essential that the presenter be knowledgeable about the learning patterns of adults.

TIPS

If you don't treat adults like adults, they will become upset, perhaps angry. In *Training Teachers,* Margie Carter and Deb Curtis offer ideas and strategies on training adults to become effective teachers. They state that "in any workshop we offer, participants have the opportunity to see things written down, hear ideas in a variety of ways from a variety of people, and move around and try things out (using methods such as props, case studies, and role plays)."[1]

In *Designing Powerful Training,* Michael Milano and Diane Ullius list six principles that must be kept in mind when training adults:

- Personal experience is the key learning tool.
- Motivation for learning is driven by needs: problem solving or personal satisfaction.
- Adults are independent learners.
- Protecting the learners' self-esteem is critical.
- Adults have clear expectations about training.
- Adults learn in a variety of ways and have preferences in learning styles.[2]

Some adults will learn best when taking notes from overhead transparencies. Others will understand a concept better after some role-playing.

Try to present the material in a variety of ways. Patience and respect are essential when teaching adults. Adults don't like to make mistakes, and they may be reluctant to ask questions. When an adult does make a mistake or ask a question, integrate these into the learning experience. Say things like, "That's a great question," or, with a mistake, "This happens all the time with PowerPoint. This is a good example. Let me mention this glitch to the class." If the workshop lasts longer than ninety minutes, work a break into the agenda. Give plenty of opportunity for the participants to practice what they learned. Be receptive of questions. Questions allow adults to get what they need from the workshop. Break the workshop into distinct sections and summarize what was learned after each section. "Okay, what did we learn?" Let the participants summarize what they just learned. Try to make some one-on-one contact with each participant, and try to make the learning experience relevant to the individual. Make it a personal experience. For example, have learners design a PowerPoint slide that reflects a hobby. If someone loves the beach, have him design a slide show around a day at the beach.

Demonstrations

DEFINITION

A demonstration is a show-and-tell program. The presenter talks about a topic while he creates something right before your eyes. An example is a program in which an origami expert explains what she's doing as she creates various animals and shapes.

PROS

Demonstrations are fun. This is the format where your imagination (and perhaps your meeting room's seating capacity) is the only limit. You can bring in a black belt expert to give a Karate demonstration. You can bring in an Italian chef to give a demonstration on making pasta. Demonstrations, when you hit on the right topic, are extremely popular. They will bring people into your library—perhaps for the first time. Demonstrations can tap into all those "how to" sections of your collection: how to cook, how to train a dog, how to dance the salsa.

CONS

The performer's fees for a demonstration can be high. Some demonstrations, such as a cooking demonstration, include materials (food, plates, silverware, etc.), and the performer will add these costs into the overall fee. You might need to distribute tickets or keep a registration list in order to regulate attendance. Insurance policies and programming policies might need to be reviewed or rewritten before you host a cooking program in which people eat the results, or a dog training program in which people bring their own dogs that might bite.

TIPS

Demonstrations can cause the occasional reality check with your programming policy and mission statement. The purpose of demonstrations is usually to relay information in an enjoyable manner. They are recreational-slash-informational. You could argue (and I believe correctly) that a wine-making demonstration is educational, but you'd probably be more accurate if you said that you were offering an informational program for the recreational wine enthusiast. If your programming policy says that you pursue recreational and informational programs, then you're all set.

You will want your presenter to be an expert on the topic. The topic itself might call for a presenter who possesses a specific, uncommon skill, such as airbrushing T-shirts. Ideally, your expert can both speak about airbrushing and *create* the T-shirts. These performers can be costly unless you can find a business owner who will perform at a reasonable price in exchange for the publicity. Or maybe you are lucky enough to have an art school down the street with faculty and students who offer demonstrations free of charge.

Live Performances

DEFINITION

Live performances are demonstrations without the talk. Examples include a play, a concert, or a ballet.

PROS

Live performances are entertaining. They can draw a crowd. They may introduce a topic to someone for the first time. And, most important, they present the material in the way that the author intended—through a human performance witnessed by an audience. A performance can be an exhilarating experience for someone who is hearing Celtic music for the first time or seeing Hamlet struggle over whether "To be, or not to be." Audience members are likely to walk right over to the information desk after the performance and ask for a copy of *Hamlet.*

CONS

As with demonstrations, you might have to give out tickets to your play or concert to ensure that two hundred people don't show up and compete for fifty seats. The musicians or actors you identify in your community might earn their living by performing at events such as library programs. Performer's fees exceeding $100 an hour are fairly common. Last, a concert of drums can be noisy; a tap dancing performance requires a hard surface. This means that certain performances require specific facilities. Make sure that the performance you have in mind is compatible with the intended site.

TIPS

Be sure that you work closely with the performers. Ask a lot of questions about their needs. What equipment will they need (such as speakers and microphones)? And try very hard to get references. Bad performances can be really, *really* bad. Bad opera or bad Shakespeare can result in someone's first and last visit with *La Bohème* or the Bard.

Discussion Groups

DEFINITION

A discussion group consists of a number of people who get together to explore something. A facilitator usually leads the group. A book discussion group is an example of this format.

PROS

Discussion groups are a great way for people to learn from other members of the community. Since the participants are library patrons and (usually) not subject experts, they feel comfortable expressing their thoughts and opinions.

People often comment afterward that the discussion caused them to think of the book or topic in a new way. Discussion groups can become mainstays in your library. The core participants of a book discussion group will faithfully arrive—with book in hand—month after month, year after year.

CONS

Discussion groups take a great deal of planning. When working with scholar-led discussion series, such as the "Choices for the 21st Century" series (see chapter 8), you will need to select the discussion topics, attend an orientation session, coordinate the program dates with the scholar, read the accompanying materials, and then perform the standard in-house paperwork and preparations. Book discussions take a fair amount of preparation as well. The books must be selected, the facilitator must read the books, and questions or discussion points must be created to stimulate the discussion. Occasionally only two or three people will show up because everyone hated, *really* hated, the book.

TIPS

Plan far in advance. If you plan to lead the discussion yourself, try to get some facilitator training. The function of a lecturer and that of a facilitator are almost exactly opposite. A lecturer talks; a facilitator gets others to talk. The Great Books Foundation (www.greatbooks.org) offers training in what it calls the Shared Inquiry method. This is a wonderful method that levels the playing field so that everyone can participate equally. The leader/facilitator poses basic questions to the group, and the group uses these questions to initiate discussion. Leaders do not offer their opinions, nor do they bring in outside materials, such as reviews. Participants are asked to support their opinions with examples from the text. This method makes everyone in the group feel equally qualified to offer insights and opinions, since no "expert" is allowed to bring in a clipping from a journal or lecture the group on his background in nineteenth-century British literature. A final tip: Make the group norms clear from the outset. For example, if you expect the participants to have read the book before the discussion, state this at the first meeting. The people who have read the book may get frustrated if you spend half the discussion summarizing the book for the one person who just checked it out five minutes ago. If the norms are to stick to the content of the book (and not to the content of a review or textbook), state this at the outset. Otherwise, you're liable to have the retired literature professor break into a monologue about how this particular book is an obvious attempt to symbolize the postmodern man through Nietzschean metaphor.

The Whole Person Catalog (www.ala.org/publicprograms) lists agencies that can help you get started with a book discussion program.[3]

Film or Video Series

DEFINITION

A film series, at the very least, involves an audience and a film. One film (or several "shorts") is usually viewed on a certain day at the same time over the course of several weeks—every Tuesday in June from 2 to 5 P.M. Film series can be thematic ("Great Silent Comedies" or "'40s Film Noir"). They can be with or without discussion. A film can be used in conjunction with other materials. For example, if the film is based on a novel, the participants could be asked to read the book beforehand. Both the film and book could then be discussed after the viewing.

PROS

Just about everyone loves films. If your library has a film collection, you may have classic films that are not yet available on video. People may tell you afterward that they hadn't seen that film since they were children. Film discussion series can be very popular. The audience does not have to prepare as they do with a book discussion.

CONS

If you are using films, be prepared for the film to break, get stuck, melt, wobble, and unravel. If you are renting a movie from your local video store, chances are that you will need to obtain public performance rights before you show it to your audience. You will need to find the firm that handles that movie's public performance rights and pay a small fee to show the video. An example of such a firm is the Motion Picture Licensing Corporation. Last, with movie theaters, television, and video stores, you have some competition out there. Consider adding an additional component to your series that might draw an audience. For example, perhaps the movie critic from the local newspaper could introduce the film.

TIPS

Try to offer a unique experience. Offer titles that are difficult or impossible to find on television or at the video store. Or, create a theme. Create a monthlong film series on Saturdays called "Saturday Afternoon Fever." Show *Grease, Saturday Night Fever, Can't Stop the Music*—all right, perhaps some of your patrons would consider this a horror series. Or, host a scholar-led film discussion series. See chapter 8 for more information on scholar-led programs. Please be sure that you are familiar with your equipment. It takes practice to learn how to work a film projector; splicing a break takes practice, too. What is the best room for the program? If the room is too large or if the floors and walls are bare, the sound might echo. Be creative with the equipment you have. If your library doesn't have a film collection and a film projector, you still might be able to get that big-screen effect. If you have an LCD projector, you can probably hook this up to your VCR and project the video onto a movie screen.

The *Whole Person Catalog* lists agencies that can help you get started with a film series.

Making Your Decision on Format

After weighing the pros and cons of each format, you will make your decision. Most of the time, the decision will be a straightforward one. A magic show can't really be anything other than a demonstration. An evening of classical guitar will fit in the live performance format. The harder decisions arise when you have a subject in mind. Let's say you want to offer a program on maintaining a healthy diet. Do you ask someone from the American Heart Association to come in and give an instructional presentation on healthy eating? Do you ask a local chef to give a cooking demonstration on the preparation of healthy dishes? There isn't a right answer. They would both be excellent programs. Perhaps you could try one of the two this year, the other next year. One thing to keep in mind, however, is the length of the program. Different programming formats tend to result in different program lengths. Lectures usually run about an hour. Discussion groups tend to run from ninety minutes to two hours. Workshops can run for several hours or days. The length of the program probably needs to be known when negotiating fees with the performer, when booking the meeting room, and when creating the flyers.

The Room and Equipment

The format you choose will affect the way you set up your meeting room. A lecture, for example, can accommodate seventy-five or more people. You will probably want to set up the room in an auditorium style, with chairs arranged in rows. Of course, the room you have available to you will also affect the format you choose. We don't all have rooms that can accommodate seventy-five people! A book discussion, however, is a much more intimate format. This calls for a round table with chairs, or just chairs alone arranged in a circle.

The size of your audience will also influence the type of equipment the performer uses to present the information. *Program Planning: Tips for Librarians* gives some guidelines to keep in mind when using projection equipment to display information to your audience.

Flip charts are recommended for audiences of fewer than 25 people.

Overhead transparencies are recommended (using at least twenty-point type) for audiences ranging from 75 to 200 people.

Slides are best with audiences ranging from small to large (25 to 200 people).

An audience up to about 25 people can clearly see a single video monitor.

LCD panels are used to project information from a computer screen or to project presentation software such as PowerPoint. These are best used with audiences ranging from 25 to 50 people.

LCD projectors are used for the same purposes as LCD panels. They have a much higher resolution, however. They are recommended for audiences ranging from 25 to 200.[4]

The formats we've discussed here are fluid. Think of them as colors on a palette. Experiment with and mix them. While someone is presenting information on common sports injuries in your meeting room, have a massage therapist in the lobby offering neck and back massages. If you have an embroidery exhibit in your display case, invite members of an embroidery club to set up a table in front of the case. The public can view the exhibit, watch experts work on embroidery projects, and ask any questions they might have. Your patrons will appreciate your creativity.

Endnotes

1. Margie Carter and Deb Curtis, *Training Teachers: A Harvest of Theory and Practice* (St. Paul, Minn.: Redleaf, 1994), 5.

2. Michael Milano with Diane Ullius, *Designing Powerful Training: The Sequential-Interactive Model* (San Francisco: Jossey-Bass/Pfeiffer, 1998), 24.

3. *The Whole Person Catalog No. 4: The Librarian's Source for Information about Cultural Programming for Adults* (Chicago: American Library Association, Public Programs Office, [1999]).

4. Gail McGovern and others, *Program Planning: Tips for Librarians* (Chicago: Continuing Library Education Network Exchange Round Table, American Library Association, 1997), 13.

10
Generating Publicity

PLANNING A PROGRAM IS A LOT LIKE PLANNING A party: You plan and plan and plan, but it's no fun unless people show up. Don't forget to invite your friends/patrons to your party/program. Create a guest list/mailing list. Send out the invitations/flyers. And then guarantee success by doubly or triply inviting people. Send mailings, followed up by phone calls and press releases. Make it appear obvious that your event is *the* event to attend.

Flyers

Let's start with the basics. Just as you create an invitation to a party, you'll create an invitation to your program. This is your flyer. Whether it will be made by hand and photocopied, created at a computer in your branch, or mass-produced in your public relations office, a flyer is essential. People are accustomed to things being announced on flyers. "Missing Cat" flyers are tacked to telephone poles, "Band Mate Wanted" flyers are posted in record stores, and "Help Wanted" flyers are taped to restaurant windows. Patrons will notice the program flyers you post on your bulletin boards and place at your information desks.

When designing a flyer, remember the following:

- Display the title of the program prominently.
- List the presenter.
- Include a brief description of the program.
- If the presenter is an author, consider including a quote from one of his or her works.
- List the day, date, and time of the program. Include a beginning and an ending time.
- List the library or libraries where the program will occur. Include the address and phone number of the library as well.
- Include your snazzy library logo.
- Include the universal symbol for wheelchair accessibility, if your library is accessible to people using wheelchairs. If you offer interpreters for the hearing impaired or other services, give patrons a telephone number they can call for further information.
- Put the word "free" on the flyer if there is no charge. Some of your patrons will always be surprised that your programs are free.
- If tickets are required for the program, mention this on the flyer.

- A cool graphic relating to the event never hurts either. The eye is always attracted to interesting images, such as clip art, a photograph of the performer, etc.

There are a few formatting decisions to make as well. Do you make a separate flyer for each branch that hosts the program, or do you make one flyer and list all the branches (and the dates and times) hosting the program? This might depend on the number of branches hosting the program and the distance between them. Someone who lives in Staten Island, New York, might not be terribly interested in knowing that the Bronx branches are hosting the same program. Some libraries list all the programs for the month on one flyer. This can result in a cluttered flyer if you do a lot of programming. If you do intend to include a lot of information, then consider a tri-fold or brochure. The brochure in figure 10.1 was created by printing on both sides of an 8½-by-11-inch piece of paper, and then folding that paper in half. The brochure includes all the young adult summer reading programs for June, July, and August.

As the attendance at your programs continues to grow, you may get to the point where you no longer need flyers. A listing in your newsletter or a single flyer posted on your bulletin board might be sufficient. This is the case with children's programs in some libraries. In such cases, a mass distribution of flyers would draw more people than the program could accommodate. Ideally, your programs will begin to draw such a constant, large number of people that flyers will become unnecessary.

Be sure to check with your state library, your state library association, and the American Library Association (www.ala.org) for sample flyers. Check these organizations' Web sites to see if they have publicity kits (with flyers) available for such events as National Library Week and Banned Books Week. They may have programming ideas as well.

Newsletters

Your newsletter is a great place to promote your programs. Just as there are those patrons who rely on flyers, there are others who use your newsletter as their guide to library events. This is particularly true if your library mails your newsletters to patrons who have asked to be placed on a mailing list. Frequently, libraries will divide the programming section of the newsletter into adult, young adult, and children's listings. The programming information you include will be similar to what you included on the flyer. You can even use the same clip art. Consider listing the names, addresses, and telephone numbers of your library branches on the back page of the newsletter. This will save space. Your programming listings will include each program's title, the description, the names of the host branches, and perhaps some clip art specific to the program. Your patrons can turn to the back of the newsletter for branch locations and telephone numbers. You can further condense the programming portion of your newsletter by including certain publicity elements only once. The library logo, the universal symbol for wheelchair accessibility (if it applies to all the program locations), the telephone number for interpreters, and the "all programs are free" reminder can take up quite a bit of space if you include them with each program listing. Instead, include them either at the beginning or end of the programming listings. Figure 10.2 contains an example of an adult programming section of a newsletter.

Mailing Lists

Now is a good time to talk about mailing lists. Your library probably already has a public relations office that maintains mailing lists. A list for programming usually includes all the local schools, colleges and universities, chambers of commerce, some local businesses and organizations, community leaders, and individuals who have requested to be placed on the list. If your library hasn't created a mailing list, then you can build one yourself (preferably using a computer program), or you can ask for help. Your chamber of commerce or economic council has resources at its disposal that allow them to generate mailing lists and labels. The software that they use may allow them to limit the data by ZIP code or business type. Ask them if they can sell this information to you as an electronic file. You can then use these data on your own computers. At the very least, they will be able to sell you the mailing labels.

FIGURE 10.1
Sample Program Flyer

★★★★ ENTERTAINMENT!

The Amazing CHADINI

Discover the mysteries of magic from ancient Egypt through Houdini. Be amazed and astounded as coins, ropes and cards defy the laws of nature.

Columbine		
Thu. 6/1 3 p.m.		

Villa	Golden	Conifer
Sat. 6/3 3 p.m.	Tue. 6/6 2 p.m.	Tue. 6/13 4 p.m.

Lakewood	Standley Lake	Daniels
Mon. 6/5 2 p.m.	Wed. 6/7 2 p.m.	Wed. 6/14 4 p.m.

Arvada	Evergreen	Edgewater
Tue. 6/6 10:30 a.m.	Thu. 6/8 10:30 a.m.	Thu. 6/15 4 p.m.

Airbrush Art
"Learn the art of airbrushing with Igor."

Exclusive showing Design and paint your own T-shirt to take home. Shirts are provided. (Limited to 20.)

Lakewood	Villa	Columbine
Mon. 6/26 10:30 a.m.	Thu. 6/29 10:30 a.m.	Mon. 7/10 11 a.m.

Evergreen	Edgewater	Golden
Tue. 6/27 10:30 a.m.	Mon. 7/3 2 p.m.	Tue. 7/11 10:30 a.m.

Daniels	Standley Lake	Arvada
Wed. 6/28 2 p.m.	Wed. 7/5 10 a.m.	Wed. 7/12 10:30 a.m.

CARTOONING basics

Artist Dave Sullivan shows how to draw cartoons from concept to finished work, then shares his tips on how to get your work published. (Limited to 20.)

NOW SHOWING at a library near you

Columbine	Evergreen	
Wed. 6/21 7 p.m.	Thu. 7/20 7 p.m.	

Villa	Arvada	Lakewood
Wed. 6/14 7 p.m.	Tue. 6/27 7 p.m.	Tue. 7/25 7 p.m.

Golden	Standley Lake	Conifer
Tue. 6/20 7 p.m.	Thu. 7/13 7 p.m.	Wed. 7/26 7 p.m.

Reading NOW THAT'S ENTERTAINMENT

Teens entering 6th to 12th grades are invited to join in a summer of fun and entertainment with the Teen Reading Club at all Jefferson County public libraries.

Read books, magazines or newspapers for a total of eight hours and earn a free paperback book. Enter the weekly contest and win the contents of the guessing jar.

Also pick up free tickets for an outstanding lineup of programs featuring magic, juggling, cartooning and airbrush art.

Sign up at the adult desk of any Jefferson County library or the bookmobile. You'll receive a card to keep track of the time you spend reading. Visit a library weekly to get your card stamped and make your guess at the guessing jar.

Your completed card will be your ticket for a free paperback at the Book Award Day in August. Books are being provided with the financial support of the Jefferson County Library Foundation.

Keep reading after you've logged your eight hours to help meet the reading challenge. If all the summer readers report at least 75,000 total hours, the foundation will donate $1,500 to HOPE Columbine Atrium and Library Fund to buy books for the new Columbine High School Library. So keep reading and help make a difference.

Get your tickets two weeks in advance for these summer features.

HEARING IMPAIRED?
Interpreters are provided upon request. Call at least one week in advance to arrange for an interpreter.
(303) 275-2205 (voice)   TTY (303) 431-2842

"Two thumbs up for fun!"

Learn to Juggle

Author, storyteller and former circus performer Angel Vigil tells about life in the circus and teaches you how to juggle. (Limited to 20.)

Conifer	Columbine	Golden
Thu. 7/6 4 p.m.	Thu. 7/18 4 p.m.	Tue. 7/25 2 p.m.

Lakewood	Villa*	Arvada
Thu. 7/13 7 p.m.	Thu. 7/20 7 p.m.	Wed. 7/26 10:30a.m.

Evergreen	Standley Lake	*This Villa program will be at the Lakewood Library.
Thu. 7/13 10:30 a.m.	Mon. 7/24 2:30	

Book Award days
FREE Paperback BOOK!

Arvada
Thu. 8/3 1-3 & 6-8 p.m.

Bookmobile 8/1-12

Columbine
Tue. 8/1 10 a.m.-2 p.m. & 6-8 p.m.

Conifer
Tue. 8/1 3-6 p.m.

Daniels
Wed. 8/2 & 9 1-5 p.m.

Edgewater
Sat. 8/5 & 12 1-4 p.m.

Evergreen
Thu. 8/3 11 a.m.-1 p.m. & 4-7 p.m.

Golden
Tue. 8/1 10 a.m.-2 p.m. & 4-7 p.m.

Lakewood
Thu. 8/3 2-4 & 6-8 p.m.

Standley Lake
Thu. 8/3 10 a.m.-noon, 2-4 & 6-8 p.m.

Villa
Tue. 8/1 10 a.m.-7 p.m.

Wheat Ridge
Thu. 8/3 11-1 & 3- 5 p.m.

OUT OF MIND
SITE RATED YA Young Adult Web Page
http://info.jefferson.lib.co.us/ya.html

FIGURE 10.2
Sample Newsletter

JULY

Especially for Adults

Administration

Thu. 20 Board of Trustees Meeting
Please call (303) 232-7114 to
confirm time and location.
7 p.m.

Foundation

Mon.10 Friends of the Library
Lakewood Library
6:30 p.m.

Columbine

Tuesday Afternoon Books
No meeting in July.

Conifer

Thu. 27 Thursday Night Book Group
Amazing Traveler,
Isabella Bird
by Evelyn Kaye
7 p.m.

Evergreen

Tuesdays Senior Read Aloud Hour
Staff reads family favorites for
senior citizens.
10:30 a.m.

Thu. 13 Thursday Night Book Group
Road to Wellville
by T. Coraghessan Boyle
7 p.m.

Exhibit Case
"Treasures from the Attic,"
antique books and letters from
the collection of David Dow

Art Exhibit
Old Evergreen from the
computer and landscapes
by Nancy Hendryx

Golden

BUFFALO BILL DAYS
USED BOOK SALE
10 a.m – 4 p.m. Sat., July 29
Noon – 4 p.m. Sun., July 30
Used books for sale in the
meeting room. Sunday is "Bag
Day" – all the books you can fit
in a bag for $2!

Lakewood

Tue. 11 Tuesday Night Books
On the Road
by Jack Kerouac
7 p.m.

Tue. 18 Family Book Group
The Great Brain
by John Dennis
For kids 8 and older.
7:30 p.m.

Tue. 25 Tuesday Afternoon Books
The Death of Artemio Cruz
by Carlos Fuentes
1 p.m.

Display Cases
Kids collections

Motorcycling in the Rockies

A motorcyclist for more than 30 years, W. Gray Buckley has
journeyed coast to coast by cycle. He's traveled in all
kinds of weather and enjoyed motorcycle camping in
most of the Rocky Mountain states.
His illustrated presentation will include the history of
motorcycling, who rides, where and why. He'll present detailed
guidelines for planning your own trip, including the itinerary,
maps, packing and safety.

7 p.m. • Tuesday, July 25 • Golden Library

7:30 p.m. • Wednesday, July 26 • Columbine Library

7 p.m. • Thursday, July 27 • Lakewood Library

2

As you build and maintain your database, look for ways to divide it into subsections. For example, do certain programs appeal to certain businesses or organizations in your service area? Can you identify certain associations, clubs, and businesses in your database that are frequently visited by seniors? If so, perhaps you can create a smaller database called "seniors." If you offer a dog training workshop, does your database allow you to limit your search to pet stores and kennels? This would allow you to write an invitation for the program and include it with those mailings that you make to the pet stores and kennels. Last, you will have to decide who gets what. For example, do you send your newsletter and flyers to everyone? Do you send flyers to everyone but the newsletter to only those who have requested it? Do you send multiple copies of your flyers to groups, such as colleges and recreation centers, that have agreed to post and distribute them? These are questions that will answer themselves, over time and through some experimentation.

Press Releases

Press releases are used to relay your programming information to newspapers and radio and television stations. The sample press release in figure 10.3 was copied from the American Library Association's Web page (www.ala.org). This sample prompts you for all the key ingredients of a press release: your library's letterhead, a catchy program title, a library contact person, and a "release" date. Many press releases have "For Immediate Release" written in bold letters right under the library letterhead. Others will have a time specified, such as "For Release after July 1." The release should be sent out at least two weeks before your program. Ideally, you will send your release to a particular contact person, or at least a particular department or office at the newspaper or television station. Most newspapers and radio and television stations will run press releases free of charge. But expect the unexpected. They might cut words from your release. They might run your releases this month but not next month. And they might run the releases a little too far in advance this month, and a little too close to the event next month. If you want more control over your pub-

licity, be sure to read the "Paid Advertising" section later in this chapter.

Public Service Announcements

Public Service Announcements (PSAs) are read on the air at television and radio stations. The key elements are very similar to those for the press release. They differ from press releases in that they specify the time needed to read them on the air, and they are written in language that appeals

FIGURE 10.3
Sample Press Release

Edit copy as needed. Retype on your library's letterhead, double-spaced. Be sure to include contact information.

FOR RELEASE NATIONAL LIBRARY WEEK
April 9–15, 2000

Contact: (name, title, phone number)

Read! Learn! Connect! @ the Library

(CITY, STATE)—It's National Library Week, a time to "Read! Learn! Connect!"

"The library has always been, and will continue to be, a one-stop shop for all your information needs," says [name and title of spokesperson]. "Whether you're checking out the latest bestseller, browsing your favorite Web site or attending a performance, the library has the resources and staff to help you find what you are looking for."

This year, the [name of library] will join libraries across the country in hosting a "Connect for Kids" Day on Saturday, April 8, to kick off National Library Week. The day will highlight the variety of resources available to kids and their families at the library and in their community. The American Library Association (ALA) is sponsoring the event in cooperation with the Benton Foundation, sponsor of a "Connect for Kids" Web site and campaign to raise public awareness about how to make the world a better place for kids, starting at the library.

The [name of library] will also offer other events to highlight library programs and services, including: [List schedule of activities.]

"National Library Week is a great time to see what's new at your local library and to get a library card if you don't have one," adds [last name]. "We encourage everyone in the community to come check us out."

For more information, including library hours, visit the [name of library] at [address], call [phone number] or see the library's Web site at [provide URL].

Source: American Library Association, www.ala.org

to the ear. The type itself should be easy to read. Consider typing the announcement in all capital letters. PSAs are also a free source of advertising, and the same adventures and inconsistencies apply to them as were mentioned with press releases. The three samples in figure 10.4 were taken from the American Library Association's Web page (www.ala.org).

Paid Advertising

Much of the publicity we've talked about so far—PSAs, press releases, mailings—can also be done as paid advertising. Why pay for it if you can get it for free? You are more likely to get what you

FIGURE 10.4
Sample Radio PSAs

PSAs should be sent to radio stations at least 4–6 weeks before National Library Week with a short cover letter. The following PSA scripts are targeted to different audiences.

ADULT
00:30

Are you interested in the Internet but have no idea how to log on and where to go once you get there? Are your kids running circles around you online? Then get connected at your local library and learn to surf the information superhighway for free. It's National Library Week, a great time to Read! Learn! Connect! @ the Library. For more information, visit the [name of library] or call [phone number]. Check us out today!

TEENS
00:30

You've got a paper due on *Romeo and Juliet* and haven't started the book yet. What do you do? Head to the library and find a quiet spot to read. Find an encyclopedia of Shakespeare's works. Listen to a performance on tape. Browse the Internet for a little more research. Didn't realize the library had everything you needed all in one spot? Think again. Read! Learn! Connect! @ the [name of library].

GENERAL
00:15

Remember when you used to walk into the library and find all those books you were just dying to read? Well, those books are still there . . . and a whole lot more. This is National Library Week, a great time to Read! Learn! Connect! @ the Library. Come see what's new today.

Source: American Library Association, www.ala.org

want, when you want it, if you pay for it. Paid publicity allows you to determine when your PSAs and news releases will run. If you want the ads to run during a particular radio show, then a paid PSA will ensure this. If you pay a newspaper to run your press release, you know that the entire release will run, uncut. You can pay for an exact piece of advertising space in the newspaper of your choice. Let's say that you decide that you want a three-by-five-inch piece of space. You can create the text, the font types, and the graphics (including your library logo) that you want to run in that space. You can then send this information to the newspaper as a camera-ready press release and they will run it as is. With paid advertising, you really do get what you pay for.

If you are fortunate enough to have an advertising budget, such a budget will allow you to try such things as renting billboard space to promote your summer programs, or renting the advertising space on the sides of buses to announce an upcoming film series. You can also conduct massive mailings. For example, you can work with a mailing house to send a letter announcing your spring programming lineup to every home within your library's ZIP code.

Direct Publicity

If you are lucky enough to work in a library system with a public relations office, you are probably getting help with the press releases, PSAs, flyers, and newsletters. On the other hand, you may be doing it yourself, along with helping your patrons at the information desk, ordering materials, writing various reports . . . and, in addition to all this, I'm about to describe one more thing that you can do yourself: direct publicity. Sometimes you can advertise your program in all three local papers and run off five thousand flyers and still have five people show up for the program. Why? Somehow you didn't tap into your target audience. Perhaps the motorcycling enthusiasts didn't attend the "Motorcycling in the Rockies" program because this group just doesn't read the "Community" section of the newspaper and didn't hear the PSA carried on National Public Radio. You might need to make a more personal contact next time you target this group.

Direct publicity involves someone making a direct contact with a person or an agency. This is usually done over the telephone. Direct publicity should begin early in the planning process. The program committee or the program coordinator should identify those programs that they think will be a tough sell. The "How to Buy a Personal Computer" program will have folks banging on your meeting room door. The "Know the Warning Signs of Alzheimer's Disease" program might need a publicity boost if it's going to attract the people who will benefit most from its message. Find a way to identify those programs that will need an additional publicity push. Comparing the program topic to the books you have on the subject is a good place to start. The circulation doesn't reveal the importance of the topic, but it does signify its popularity. People are attracted to the materials and programs that cover popular topics. Other topics might need a little promotion in order for them to get the attention that they deserve.

Once you've identified a program that will need additional publicity, assign someone the task of identifying groups or people in the area that might be interested in attending the program. Are you presenting a program on how to drive cross-country on a motorcycle? Are you concerned that the turnout might be low? If yes, then check your local, state, and national directories, such as the *Encyclopedia of Associations,* to see which motorcycling associations exist in your area.[1] You probably also have a local directory of clubs and societies. Does a nearby college offer a course on motorcycle repair? Check the phone book for motorcycle dealerships. Jot down the telephone numbers of the associations, clubs, businesses, and colleges that might be able to help you with your publicity efforts. This information needs to be gathered at least three weeks before the program. When you get within three weeks of the program, it's time to place the call.

Figure 10.5 is a form that you can use when placing your calls. The form will give you some talking points to refer to as you describe your program over the telephone. It can also be mailed or faxed to the groups you have identified. If you are speaking to people on the telephone, be sure to ask them if they can promote your program to their students, customers, or members. The attendance at a particular program will go up dramatically if you can get a professor or club president to announce your program to the students or members. Also ask them if they can distribute your flyers. If they say yes, mail the flyers to their attention, or ideally, offer to hand-deliver the flyers to your contact person.

FIGURE 10.5
Talking Points for Direct Publicity

Hello, my name is [Name] and I'm a librarian at [My Library]. Our library offers a variety of programs for children and adults. I'd like to tell you about an upcoming program.

Program Title: _____

_____

Presenter: _____

_____

Of interest to: _____

_____

Description of presentation (content, visuals, audience interaction—what the audience will see and hear): _____

_____

_____

_____

Why the Library is offering this program: _____

_____

_____

_____

_____

Locations hosting the program:

Library_____   Address _____
Telephone _____
Time: From _____to _____   Day/Date _____

Library_____   Address _____
Telephone _____
Time: From _____to _____   Day/Date _____

Library_____   Address _____
Telephone _____
Time: From _____to _____   Day/Date _____

Library_____   Address _____
Telephone _____
Time: From _____to _____   Day/Date _____

Library_____   Address _____
Telephone _____
Time: From _____to _____   Day/Date _____

Library_____   Address _____
Telephone _____
Time: From _____to _____   Day/Date _____

Tickets required: _____ YES   _____ NO

For tickets, call the library at which you'd like to attend the program.

Library contact: _____   Phone:_____

Odds and Ends

There are a few other things that can help you get the word out to your patrons. Sometimes the little things count the most. I've coordinated book discussion groups that were advertised in newspapers, in our newsletter, and on flyers that were distributed throughout the library system. But on more than one occasion, only a handful of people had signed up as the day of the discussion approached. A few days before the discussion, I always placed a stack of flyers on the information and checkout desks, and I asked the circulation staff to give a flyer to each person who went through the checkout line. The number of names on the sign-up sheet always jumped just before the discussion. I believe this is at least partially because of the in-branch publicity that was done during the week or so before the discussion.

So, without further ado, here's a list of miscellaneous things you can do to increase the likelihood that your patrons will notice and attend your program:

- Consider whether your program can be viewed as a human-interest story. Is a popular or intriguing community figure presenting the program? If so, write the human-interest story and submit it as a press release three weeks or so before the program.
- Place flyers at all service desks.
- Two or three days before the program, ask the circulation staff to include a flyer with the materials they check out to your patrons.
- Order some plastic stands that can vertically display a copy of your flyer.
- Place flyers in the library windows the day of the program. Write "Today!" across the tops of the flyers.
- Announce upcoming programs during your introduction of the current program.
- Create a colorful banner for your program and hang it on the outside of your building.

Write a review or summation of the program immediately after it occurs. Publish this in the library newsletter, and consider sending this as a press release to the local newspapers. This won't help the attendance at your program, but it might increase the attendance at the next branch that is offering the same program.

Notes from the Field

Frequently, as I wrote this book, I turned to peers for advice, or just for a reality check, to make sure that I was on the right track. To hear from as many people as possible, I formed a virtual discussion group of librarians from around the United States who had an interest in or involvement with adult programming. When I was planning this chapter on publicity, I e-mailed the group and asked them what types of publicity they used in their libraries. Susan Akers, a librarian with the Anderson (Ind.) Public Library, responded with some extremely insightful comments. She also included a yearlong publicity calendar. The calendar struck me as a terrific idea. Both her comments and the calendar are included in figures 10.6 and 10.7.

In this chapter, we've looked at some techniques you can use to get your programs noticed by your patrons. Over the course of the last ten chapters, we've explored policies, budgets, demographics, topics, target audiences, formats, performers, and publicity. It's getting very close to show time. We have a little time yet before the curtain rises. Let's move forward then with our final preparations.

Endnote

1. *Encyclopedia of Associations: Regional, State, and Local Organizations* (Detroit, Mich.: Gale, published annually).

FIGURE 10.6
Publicity Tips

Review your library logo. Is it old/outdated? Work with a professional designer to brainstorm a new look. Libraries need to break out of the stereotype of only promoting books in the design element of their logos. I wouldn't recommend having a logo-design contest, though. They aren't generally very good and make for poor community relations for the ones whose designs don't win!

Take a walk through the library with fresh eyes. Is the signage ragged/old-looking? The inside and outside of the facility should be neat and clean with no trash, and should be as clutter-free as possible. Flyers, etc., should be placed in information racks or in plastic holders that keep them from blowing around and becoming litter in the building. Display areas should be used to promote various displays and stay interesting and exciting! We're a visually oriented society and as such enjoy looking at neat displays!

Renew relationships with local reporters, editors. This is one of your best resources to reach the community. Submit news releases (well written and according to standard guidelines) on a regular basis. They usually prefer it by faxing; don't generally call the reporter to see if "they received the news release." If you used the correct address and/or fax number, they received it. They may not always use it, but if it was sent in a reasonable time frame, and is newsworthy and well written, they will be more apt to use it.

Try to participate in information fairs, home shows, senior events, etc., that give you a chance to promote the library "on the road" through being out in the public eye.

Source: Susan Akers, Anderson (Ind.) Public Library

FIGURE 10.7
Publicity Calendar

JANUARY—Call or write to local service clubs, Rotary/Exchange/Optimist, etc., and get the director on the speaking circuit in the community. Create a display with books and videos promoting "New Beginnings" that focuses on New Year's resolutions (improve marriage communication/weight issues/finances/stress management/physical fitness/slowing down/getting in control of one's life/parent-teen communication). Invite a speaker on a popular topic.

FEBRUARY—Black History Month. Promote and celebrate culture/history. Create programming that will attract people that don't otherwise visit the library. Brainstorm for creative programming for April.

MARCH—Improve or build on relationship with your Friends group. Brainstorm activities and promotion of library for April's National Library Week. March (Women's History Month) is an excellent time to promote library resources on that topic. Travelogues on trips to New Zealand, Hawaii, Alaska, and Australia are always good this time of year. Find someone in your community, a retired teacher perhaps, with good speaking skills who has traveled and can discuss highlights of the trip as well as what to know about/plan for before the trip. We always have thirty to forty people at these types of programs.

APRIL—Invite your contact with the local newspaper to visit and write a story highlighting the community's use of the library. Thank your Friends during National Volunteer Week and hold a reception for them with punch and cookies, etc. This allows staff from various departments to bring cards and notes of thanks to the Friends for their work throughout the previous year.

MAY—Hold a gardening program (or can be done in late March or early April)—these types of "how to" programs always attract people.

JUNE—Book a traveling display that will be of interest to your community. The state's historical society usually has high-quality displays for loan.

JULY—Assess your library's signage, print material, flyers, etc. Are they left up past their date? Get rid of handwritten signs and use only computer-generated signs for a professional look. Your library's guide should be given out to every new library customer and be an overview of what the library offers, complete with phone numbers and short blurbs describing each department. Your print material should always look nice/professionally done with an up-to-date, exciting logo highly visible.

AUGUST—Make a list of community and/or church groups in your district to which you can submit short blurbs to promote the library services and/or events periodically. Send them things periodically! Try to work with local schools to be on hand for kindergarten sign-up at the schools. Parents can get kids their library card at the school's site that day also!

SEPTEMBER—Look for opportunities to piggyback with universities for speakers and authors. This can cut down costs and make speaker fees more affordable.

OCTOBER—Begin planning the following year's budget. Set aside budget money for promotional, inexpensive items, such as magnets, pens, and pencils. These go a long way—especially magnets with the library logo and phone number with hours.

Source: Susan Akers, Anderson (Ind.) Public Library

11
Producing the Program

Finally, the time has come to host your program. Let's assume that as you begin this chapter, your program is about three weeks from today. There isn't much left to do. Someone (probably you) has taken responsibility for coordinating the program. A topic has been chosen. You've found a performer and agreed on the topic, fee, and format. You've chosen a location, date, and time. You've submitted the required paperwork, requesting publicity and the necessary equipment. During the planning you did for the publicity, you also decided whether you would require tickets or preregistration. Everything looks good and in order. Are we forgetting anything?

The Anderson (Ind.) Public Library produced the checklist included in figure 11.1. You probably completed the items in the "Arrangements" section months ago. If you see any tasks here that still need to be done, you will have just enough time to complete them—even with only three weeks remaining—before the program occurs.

Pre-event

The checklist in figure 11.1 covers all you need to do immediately before and after your program. Let me elaborate on a few of the other items included in the checklist. For some last-minute publicity ideas, please refer to chapter 10. Program evaluations will be covered in chapter 12. The speaker confirmation is the heart of this checklist. Try to call your speaker three weeks before the program occurs. This is your final chance to make sure that you and the speaker are on the same page. Verify all the dates, times, and locations. Let him know that you will fax, e-mail, or mail the directions to him. Explain to him when and where he can collect his check. Many libraries like to pay the speaker after the performance. This gives the speaker an extra incentive to appear. This is also your opportunity to verify all the speaker's needs. Make sure that you are clear on what equipment he needs. Which pieces of equipment will the library supply? What equipment will the speaker bring with him? Will he supply the slide projector and you will supply the screen? Let the speaker know if he will be asked to use any assistive devices, such as the microphone to an FM personal hearing system. After you verify the equipment with the speaker, double-check to see that you have requested everything that is needed. What materials will the speaker distribute to the audience? Make sure that you are both in agreement as to who will make the photocopies. Will the speaker drop the originals by your library for you to copy?

Although you probably discussed the target audience with the speaker several months ago, you should briefly discuss the audience again on the telephone. The two of you should try to estimate the number of people who will attend the program. This will help you decide how to set up for the program. Will you use auditorium-type seating, expecting a large audience, or will you set up the chairs in a circle, expecting a smaller, more interactive audience? Does the speaker want a table to himself? The room configuration can greatly affect the tone of the program. Circular seating, for example, sets the tone for a discussion, not a lecture.

FIGURE 11.1
Hosting a Program   Checklist

ARRANGEMENTS

Okay program with department manager _____

Get date of event and room booked with appropriate library staff _____

Decide room arrangements: chairs/tables/lectern, equipment, microphone, etc. _____

Create purchase order for honorarium _____

PRE-EVENT

Confirm with speaker date, time, etc. _____

Give directions by fax to speaker _____

Prepare your introduction of speaker _____

Rehearsal (visually "walk through" your program—check timing) _____

Decide the type and location of microphones _____

Room size adequate—not too large is best _____

Book sale table (where/who's in charge?) _____

Arrange to escort speaker into room, if applicable _____

Other: Use purchase order to purchase food, program supplies, etc. _____

PUBLICITY

Promote through library newsletter/create display in library if possible _____

Review speaker bios to prepare a good introduction _____

Send photo of speaker and/or news release of event to local media _____

Promote event through Public Service Announcements (if applicable) _____

Posters, flyers, newspaper, radio, cable, special audiences, mailings to clubs _____

PRINTED NEEDS FOR PROGRAM

Copy handouts, if any _____

Set up a table in room where program is located that promotes library resources on the topic _____

GUEST DETAILS

Hotel or bed-and-breakfast arrangements have been made with financial arrangements _____

Airport pickup or check to see if he or she already has directions to library _____

AT END OF EVENT

Put up library resources _____

Collect evaluation cards, read, give to Community Relations for adding to database _____

List successes and challenges, evaluate event, and put in file _____

By now the flyers for the program should be printed and available to the public. Let the speaker know that you can mail him a copy. Ask him if he'd like several flyers to distribute to friends, clubs, and local businesses. Ask him if he would like you to introduce him. If he would, then ask him to give you two or three pieces of information about himself that he would like to have included in the introduction. Offer to fax or e-mail the introduction to him before the program occurs. You might want to wrap up the telephone call by informing him of anything that you think might affect him during the performance. Will you have an interpreter on hand? If yes, then let him know, only because he should know that he will be sharing the stage with someone else. Also, make sure that you verify that the interpreter will be present at your program. Will you serve refreshments? This can cause some commotion at the beginning of the program. If you decide to serve snacks, the speaker should be told that there will be some conversations and networking among the audience before the program begins. Before you hang up, it doesn't hurt to let the performer know how much you and your patrons are looking forward to the program. Not all performers have experienced the enthusiasm of an audience of library patrons!

After your telephone call and before your program, you have a few loose ends to wrap up. You will be following through with your obligations to the speaker. You'll be mailing the library locations and directions to him, along with copies of the flyers. You'll be verifying equipment, including the necessary tables and chairs. Who will present the check to the speaker? Has the check already been drafted? Do you need to make any photocopies before the program? How is the speaker's introduction coming along? Have you sent him a copy?

If your program relies on the help of others, verify with these people as well. Give the sign language interpreter a call. Give your caterer a call to verify the delivery time of the lunches. Does the library staff have the information they need to explain the details of the program to someone on the telephone or in person? If your program has any special components, such as preregistration or accompanying reading materials, make sure that the staff understand how to register people and distribute the materials. If you are charging an attendance fee, do staff know the details about how the money will be collected? Will you accept checks? Who should the check be made out to? These are questions your patrons will ask. You can help your coworkers by typing up some instructions that will help them make the program a success. Double-check your own schedule to make sure that you will be working the day or evening of the program. If not, hopefully you can find a coworker who can introduce the speaker, set up a book display in the room, and distribute and collect the evaluations. Ideally, you will be able to give the introduction, the books, and the evaluation forms to your coworker in advance. And, finally, ask yourself whether you can do everything yourself the day of the program. Do you need someone to collect tickets while you make last-minute preparations with the speaker? Perhaps you should consider scheduling a library page or volunteer to work part of the program with you.

The Contingency Plan

What do you do if the performer cancels, or worse, just doesn't show up? Rather, what do you do after your initial hysteria subsides? In the literature I've read while writing this book, I've come across some authors who advise that the library have a backup plan in place. The implication in these articles and books seems to be that the program coordinator should actually have an alternate *program* ready, in the wings. This seems a bit far-fetched. I just can't imagine finding an alternate performer who is willing to appear at each program in case the original performer cancels. It also seems unrealistic to expect a staff person to step in and improvise an entire program.

Having a contingency *plan* in place, however, is always a good idea. The same plan can then be used for all cancellations. If your library maintains a programming manual, you could place this plan there for staff to locate in the event of a cancellation. Or staff could be introduced to the plan during a programming workshop. Whatever plan you devise, it will probably be relatively brief and straightforward. It could be as simple as:

1. Let the audience know that the program has been canceled.

2. If there is a reason, such as the performer being ill, let the audience know.

3. Apologize.

4. Let the audience know if the program will be held at other locations in the near future.

5. If you have the staff to follow through, ask for the names and telephone numbers of the audience members. Tell them that you will call them and let them know if you can reschedule the performer at your location.

6. Tell the audience about other upcoming library programs and events.

7. Offer to give them a tour of the library or take them to the materials in the library that relate to the program topic.

8. Apologize.

Show Time!

All your work is about to bear fruit. The few hours before the program will be spent with housekeeping tasks—setting up equipment, arranging tables and chairs, etc. You will probably set up a display of related library materials in the program's meeting room. You will set the program evaluations, flyers for upcoming programs, and other handouts on the chairs. (If you have not yet developed patron and staff evaluation forms, you might want to jump ahead to chapter 12.) Walk around the branch and remind all the staff of the program and its room location. This will help them field last-minute questions from patrons. As the start time approaches, a glass of water will be set aside for the speaker. A staff person will show people to the meeting room as they arrive. This staff person will also collect any tickets or admission fees.

When the speaker arrives, show her the room setup. Remind her that you've written an introduction for her, and verify that she does want to be introduced. Many performers prefer to introduce themselves. If she wants to introduce her-self, ask her if she could also point out the table of library materials to the audience. Also, ask the performer to ask the audience to fill out their evaluation forms. If you do introduce the performer, then point out the evaluation forms and materials beforehand, and also announce any upcoming library programs. Then introduce the performer and let her do her stuff.

Before we move on, let's pause a moment and enjoy the program. If you can attend the entire program, do it. Even if it involves rearranging your schedule or calling in a substitute, try to attend the program. Staffing situations probably will prevent you from attending all the programs that you coordinate, but at the very least, pop in and out of the room and catch what you can. The first, and admittedly bureaucratic, reason for doing so is to view firsthand the quality of the performer's presentation skills and the program's content. This will allow you to write a staff evaluation of the program. The second reason is far more personal: A library program is an incredible experience. Not only do you get to immerse yourself in the performance, you also get to witness the audience as they learn and laugh and listen to one another. Programs energize your audiences. They'll energize you, too. Sometimes we can get lost in the planning and the procedures. When you actively attend a program, you can't help but think, "Yeah, this is why we do this." Reward yourself. It'll keep you in touch with your desired result: quality programs for your patrons.

After the program, thank the performer and, if you have it, hand over the check! Write down the number of people who attended the program. Many libraries and branches submit program attendance figures in a monthly report. And last, if time permits, glance at the patron evaluation forms and write your evaluation of the program while it is still fresh in your mind.

Wrap Up

There's not much left to do now. The big event is over. It's like waking up the day after hosting a New Year's Eve party. The room needs to be cleaned and set back to its original layout. At least with a New Year's party, people send you thank-you cards. When you host a library program, you are the one writing the thank-you cards. But it isn't so bad. Your performer did a terrific job and it's a sincere way to show your and your patrons' appreciation. You might even want to quote or paraphrase some patrons' comments to show how much the audience enjoyed the program. Pop the card in the mail. Now you can spend some time with the patron evaluations. Did the patrons like the performer? Did they say that the content was good? Did they suggest future programs? How many of your patrons have simply written "Thank you" in the "comments" section? Check to see if you are supposed to send these evaluation forms to your program committee or public relations office. If yes, put them in the interoffice mail. We'll have a closer look at evaluating programs in the next chapter, but first . . .

Pause . . . and take the time to congratulate yourself and those involved for a job well done.

12
Evaluating
the Program

So, how did you do? Let's hear from you and your patrons. Gather up those audience program evaluations and look them over. They will help you determine whether the program was beneficial to your community. The staff program report—the form *you* fill out—will help determine whether the program was cost-effective.

The Audience Evaluation

Let's begin with your patrons' perspectives. What did they tell you on the evaluations? What did you ask them? Most audience program evaluations seem to be a cross between a demographic questionnaire and a program evaluation. This makes sense. You want to know what your patrons thought about the program, yet you also want to know if the program reached its intended target audience. The trick is achieving a balance. If you ask too many demographic questions, such as a patron's age and sex, then you have less opportunity to ask questions about the program itself. And expanding the evaluation form won't help you. If it exceeds one page, people are much less likely to fill it out.

Most audience program evaluations contain a few key elements. They ask the patron to rate the content of the program. The patron can be asked to rate the content as poor, fair, average, good, and excellent. Or, the patron might be asked to rate the content on a scale from 1 to 5. The audience program evaluation can also ask the patron to rate the performer on his skills or presentation style. The patron may also be asked to rate the accompanying materials, such as bibliographies and other resources. In order for you to learn which forms of publicity are effective, the evaluation should ask patrons how they learned about the program—through the library newsletter, a flyer, the newspaper, etc. The evaluation should give patrons an opportunity to suggest future programming topics. You will also be surprised at the number of adult patrons that comment on the environment—the lighting, the seating, the acoustics of the room. You might want to include a question that allows the patron to comment on the comfort level of the room.

In the preceding paragraph, we began to construct an audience program evaluation that asks patrons some questions about the performer, the program's content, the publicity, and the meeting room. We haven't, however, asked the patrons anything about themselves. Do you want to know the overall age of the audience? Is it important to know if more men or women attended the program? Do you want to know which branches your audience visits most frequently? Perhaps you want to ask each patron if this is the first time she has visited the library. This question, for example, could help you determine if the program attracted first-time users to the library. Such questions help you determine if you've reached a particular target audience. Just remember that no one wants to sit and fill out a long questionnaire after a program. Try to keep it short. Ask the questions that are most important to you. In a moment, we'll explore how you can answer some of these demographic questions through the staff program report (instead of placing them on the evaluation that your patrons will complete).

Before moving on, take a look at the audience program evaluation in figure 12.1.

The Staff Program Report

Ideally, the person who planned the program will be able to view all or part of it. If this isn't possible, try to schedule another staff person to at least pop into the program for a few minutes. Library staff know a quality program when they see one. And they recognize when things go off track. Their input is crucial if you are going to get a solid, overall view of the performer and the material she or he presents. They will relay this input by completing a staff program report.

Be sure to use your staff program reports to their best advantage. Some demographic-type questions can be placed on the staff program report instead of on the audience program evaluation. For example, many audience evaluations ask each patron to mark an age range—under 17, 17–25, 25–40, 40–55, and 55 and older. Patrons are also asked to mark whether they are male or female. You can pose all these questions to your audience and still end up with data that are difficult to use. For example, if you host a program that is targeted toward single moms, a staff person may have to sort through the audience evaluations and try to guess—based on the age and sex

of the audience—whether the program reached the target audience. You can probably, however, get better data by having a staff member observe the audience. Construct your staff program report in a way that asks the right questions. You can include a line on the staff report that asks the staff member to identify the target audience. The staff member can then look around the room and mark on another line whether the intended target audience was reached.

Let's say that your program "Single Moms: Getting through the First Six Months" is primarily targeted toward, surprise, single moms. You are probably hoping that the audience will include at least a few single moms. During the program, you can look around the room and note the number of women in the audience who appear to be single moms. (Admittedly, this will take some guesswork.) You can then summarize this information in the "Was the target audience reached?" section of your program report. The fewer demographic questions you ask your audience, the more space they will have on their evaluations to answer questions about the performer and the program content.

As you begin to create the document that will become your staff report, try to keep a few things in mind. The report should combine several factors. It will summarize the patrons' responses to the program. It will include the staff person's comments about the program. It will document the amount of staff time that went into planning, promoting, and executing the program. The amount of time and resources will be compared to the number of people who attended the program and their reactions to the performer and the content.

After you've created your staff program report, you will have to remind staff to use it. And the report really does need to be completed while the program is still fresh in their mind. Encourage the staff to sit down, whenever possible, and complete the report right after the completion of the program. Figure 12.2 shows a sample staff program report.

Programming is, in ways, a collection development process. Just as staff determine the desirability of library materials, they also have the responsibility of determining the quality of

FIGURE 12.1
Audience Program Evaluation

AUDIENCE PROGRAM EVALUATION

Date: _____ Branch: _____ Program Title: _____

Overall how would you rate this program:

            poor   fair   good   very good   excellent

How would you rate the speaker on:

   Knowledge of the subject: poor   fair   good   very good   excellent

   Presentation: poor   fair   good   very good   excellent

What did you like best about the program:

What did you like least about the program:

Is this the first time you have attended a library program?   Yes   No

Would you be interested in attending future library programs?   Yes   No
   If "No", why not?

   If "Yes", what other topics would you like to see discussed?

How did you hear about this program? (Check all that apply)

   ❑ Library Newsletter   ❑ Television (Station name: _____)

   ❑ Library staff   ❑ Newspaper (Newspaper name: _____)

   ❑ Library web site   ❑ Radio (Station name: _____)

   ❑ Library flier   ❑ From a friend

   ❑ Other: _____

Circle branches of Jefferson County Public Library you regularly use:

   Arvada   Belmar   Bookmobile   Columbine   Conifer   Daniels

   Edgewater   Evergreen   Golden   Lakewood   Standley Lake   Wheat Ridge

Do you have a Jefferson County Public Library card?   Yes   No

Additional comments/suggestions:

Staff: Please return completed form to the Chair of the Program Committee.

— —

Would you like to receive a copy of the library's newsletter by mail?   Yes   No
   If "Yes", please write your

   Name _____

   Address _____

   City _____ Zip Code _____

Source: Jefferson County (Colo.) Public Library

FIGURE 12.2
Staff Program Report

STAFF PROGRAM REPORT

Program coordinator complete this section before sending to branch.

Program Coordinator for JCPL _____

Program title _____

Intended target audience _____

Program description (include length of program):

Publicity received from PIO _____

_____

Hours spent: planning _____   promoting _____

To be completed by branch staff

Name _____ Date _____ Branch _____

Publicity done by branch _____

_____

Branch setup time _____

Library Resources (list material used during program – book displays, videos, bibliographies):

Equipment (list equipment used and if there were any problems):

Number in audience: Adults _____ Teens _____ Children _____

Was intended target audience reached?   Yes   No

Audience evaluations/reaction:

Your comments:

Please send white copy of completed form, along with Audience Program Evaluations, to the Chair of the Program Committee
yellow copy - Program Coordinator   pink copy - Branch File

_____

Source: Jefferson County (Colo.) Public Library

library programs. Look at the staff program reports very carefully. Ask yourself many of the same questions you ask yourself when ordering or deselecting a book or video. Is the information accurate? Does the item/performer cover the materials it purports to cover? Is the production value high? Is the quality as good or better than other, similar items/performers? Is the price reasonable? Most performers create wonderful programs that impress both the audience and the staff. Rarely do you get an inferior program. But when you do, you must make the tough decision about whether you should ask the performer back or whether you should seek a replacement.

What Does It All Mean?

Now that you have collected the evaluations, it's a natural impulse to look them over carefully, perhaps share them with your coworkers, and then file them snugly away in a three-ring binder called "Program Evaluations." They will stay untouched in that binder until the paper itself biodegrades. Please don't let these evaluations be looked at once and then fall into a void. It *is* a good idea to keep some type of file—three-ring or otherwise—that tracks programs. This database will consolidate information you have gathered from your patrons and staff. This file, whether on paper or in a spreadsheet, can track the performer, what he or she did, how many patrons attended the performance, the cost, equipment needed, and excerpts from patron comments. In the future, staff who are looking for certain types of programs can use this file. Staff can identify a performer who has presented a specific topic that received positive comments from patrons. If there are budget limitations, the file can help here as well. A sample file, created on Excel, is included in figure 12.3.

Another file or list that can develop from the evaluation forms is a simple wish list from your patrons. Keep a list of what they say they would like to see as future programs. You will be surprised at how many clever ideas your patrons come up with. And this will help take some of the guesswork out of your future programming.

The staff and audience evaluation forms really are surveys. Your patrons and staff have told you how you are doing with your programming efforts. They can be powerful tools to refer to when you are seeking funding from your library foundation or any funding source. You can create a presentation that includes the number of people who attended your programs, opinions about the programs and performers, suggestions for future programs, and actual patron comments. Include a few comments in your presentation. Look through the past few months' evaluations. You will find such gems as "Wonderful program! The woman who came to do the program was *very* good," or "What a fun program! Wish you could have more of them!" These comments show your funders that they will be backing a winner when they contribute to future library programs.

Negative Comments

What do you do with the negative comments? These comments will have just as much weight as the positive comments. On a rare occasion you will sponsor a program that elicits several negative comments. Hopefully your evaluation form will ask the questions that help you to determine if the topic was the problem, or the presentation style, or the size of the room. Sometimes, if you notice negative comments early enough, you can fix the problem before the same program is held again at another location. Perhaps patrons are telling you that a performer is shamelessly plugging his lawn care business during his presentation on garden pests. You can probably fix this by calling the performer and asking him to tone this down at his next program. If a patron is offended by a program topic, this should probably be handled in a manner that parallels your reconsideration procedure for library materials. You will want to begin by providing the patron with a copy of your programming policy. Offer a comment card. Let the patron explain her or his concerns about the program, either verbally or in writing. You might be able to offer a better response if you listen to the patron's comments and offer to telephone or write a response to the patron within a specified number of days. You are allowed to give

FIGURE 12.3
Adult Programming Database

NAME	ADDRESS AND PHONE	TAX # OR SS #	WHAT THEY DO	AVG. STATUS	ATTEND.	COST	EQUIPMENT	COMMENTS
Dan Daniels	The Greasy Grill 123 Four St. Denver, CO 80220 (303) 111-1111	000-11-2222	Holiday eating tips, nutrition, and controlling holiday binges	Request Approved	32	$125	None from the library	Positive reviews from both patrons and staff. "What a wonderful program to have during the holidays! Thank you!" Many patrons asked that the program be repeated next year. Enjoyed by a wide range of age groups (mix of men and women).
John Johnson	6 Seven Circle Castle Rock, CO 80104 (303) 222-2222	123-45-6789	Victorian sojourn	Request Approved	20	$125	None from the library	Rave reviews from patrons and staff. "Very delightful and informative and entertaining." Presenter used a number of props, costumes, cooking, etc. Patrons suggested that he come back for other programs. Enjoyed by a wide range of age groups (mostly female).
Patty Patterson	1234 Fifth Way Boulder, CO 80302 (303) 123-4567		An evening with Patty Patterson	Request Approved	26	$0	Slide projector	Audience enthusiastic per staff evaluation. "A great way to promote poetry reading." Patron and staff requests for more programs on similar topics (i.e., author readings and/or signings).

yourself some time to formulate your thoughts. It's okay to say, "Thank you for your comments. Do you mind if I find out more information about this and get back to you by Thursday?" Your next step might be to take a look at letters that have been sent to patrons who commented on materials in the collection. These letters usually:

Thank the patron for his or her comments.

Restate the patron's concern.

State that a staff member has reviewed the material.

Summarize the content of the material.

Offer excerpts of reviews from professional journals.

Relate how the material fits within the library's collection development policy and/or mission statement.

State whether, based on the preceding factors, you will continue to keep the material in your collection.

Remind the patron that staff are always available to provide help when selecting materials.

Thank the patron for his or her comments and for using the library.

Offer the patron a name and telephone number of someone in administration who can be contacted if the patron would like to continue to pursue the matter.

Unless you are offering a photography workshop on the wonders of Mapplethorpe, you will probably never have a patron pursue a complaint with a program. If it does happen, however, refer to your materials reconsideration process as a guideline. Since most programs occur once or just a few times and then disappear, the chances of someone lodging a formal complaint are fairly slim. Most people who pursue such things usu-

ally want an item removed from the collection. This automatically occurs with a program: there is a performance, and then the event is over.

At the Very Least

Perhaps you don't have the time to hand out patron evaluations during the program and fill out staff reports afterward. At the very least, take a head count at each program. Write down the name of the program and the attendance. If at some point someone asks you for a status report, then you can generate a simple report that lists the programs that you have hosted and the attendance figures. Program attendance figures can be used to create a variety of persuasive statistics. *Output Measures for Public Libraries* gives some guidance on how you can generate statistical data by using your program attendance figures.[1] For example, you can calculate the annual program attendance, the average attendance per program, and the program attendance per capita. You could also look at the attendance of particular types of programs, such as film series, book discussions, etc.

Receiving and reading evaluation forms can be a delight. It's like receiving a thank-you card after hosting a party. The responses are nearly always positive. The forms have a way of bringing you full circle. You see which programs were huge successes, and you get suggestions for future programs. And this gets you to thinking about what you will offer next. The planning begins anew.

Endnote

1. Nancy A. Van House and others, *Output Measures for Public Libraries,* 2nd ed. (Chicago: American Library Association, 1987), 71–72.

13
Looking toward the Future of Adult Programming

BEFORE I BEGAN WRITING THIS BOOK, I POSTED A message to the electronic mailing list *PUBLIB*.[1] I asked my peers to tell me what they would like to see included in a book on adult programming. They gave me many wonderful suggestions. One particularly interesting suggestion was to include some information on where adult programming was headed. Prognosticating sounded like fun, so I decided to work this into the book. Knowing, however, that I did not possess any divination powers, I again turned to my peers for help. I sent a second posting to *PUBLIB:*

> Hello. I am currently writing a book for the American Library Association on adult programming. I will soon be writing a chapter entitled "Looking toward the Future of Adult Programming." It will be a chapter that tries to prognosticate where adult programming in libraries is headed. It will include programming topics that will likely be popular in the future (such as computer-skills classes), formats (lectures, performances, etc.), and ways to deliver these programs (via the Web, television, live at the library, etc.). I'll probably also talk about how more and more libraries are

partnering with other local agencies—even combining facilities (such as libraries and police stations, and libraries and schools sharing facilities). These partnerships will affect the types of programs that libraries offer. I'll also talk about how the price of quality performers is increasing rapidly, which will lead libraries to seek more and more help from outside funding sources.

> If you have any thoughts on the future of adult programming, even if it's one sentence or a paragraph, I'd love to include them in the book. I will be happy to acknowledge you and your library.

> Thanks for your help.

I received several responses. The creative programming that is taking place out there is just amazing. And equally amazing is the enthusiasm of the people who are doing the programming. Many people thought that adult programming would evolve over time, but no one said that she or he saw it becoming less important. Here is what folks had to say.

Role of the Library in the Future

Many people spoke about the library becoming much more of a community center in the future.

> I think one of the things that will develop is that libraries will be more of a community center for mutual learning, and that we will find ways to cooperate with other agencies like Community Education departments and local schools, to tap into local "experts" at low cost.
>
> —Ann Hokanson
> Prescott (Wisc.) Public Library

> I believe that the public library role of "Community Activities Center" is frequently overlooked for adults.
>
> —Hillary Theyer
> Torrance (Calif.) Public Library

> Several Wisconsin public libraries have incorporated the concept of becoming a community center into their long-range plans. Adult programs are a key way to attract patrons to the library as community center. . . . Adult programming will survive into the future because the programs are an important way for individuals to socialize and to continue their lifelong learning goals. I think they have to be directed by librarians because they have the skills to organize, market, and conduct the programs.
>
> —Cecilia Wiltzius
> Appleton (Wisc.) Public Library

> I firmly hope our library will be considered a "cultural gathering place" in the future.
>
> —Carol Ann Robb
> Pittsburg (Kans.) Public Library

Many people spoke about how partnerships would continue to be important. By partnering with other groups in our service areas, we are ensuring that we will continue to connect with our target audiences.

> Each year I try to target a new market/segment by cooperative ventures with local organizations. This helps me build audiences and provides volunteers to assist with program night.

> Heritage Society, Photo Club, VFW, Woman's Club, writing groups, area publishers, book groups, and local universities are some examples of our successful partnership.
>
> —Susan Emmons-Kroeger
> Lisle (Ill.) Library District

Libraries will also have to continue to keep pace with the ways our patrons prefer to receive their information. Overdue notices and other notices are now sent to patrons via e-mail. It looks as if some patrons now or soon will prefer receiving library publicity that way, too.

> More of our publicity information for our programs is going out now electronically. We publicize on our Web site. Also recently we sent information by mail to local writing groups publicizing an author signing. One asked for me to please e-mail the information so that she could in turn send it on to her whole group!
>
> —Janet Bergeron
> Oldsmar (Fla.) Public Library

Topics of the Future

These comments were fun to read. The respondents were aware of the growing senior population. They saw that this would affect the types of programs that are offered in the future, but they also recognized that libraries would be able to call on these folks as potential performers. The "community center" thread continues here. Libraries can further explore ways to unite the community by bringing individuals into contact with various agencies. For example, doctors can come to the library and offer health screenings for patrons. And people will increasingly look to the library to teach them the skills they need to be successful in society. I'll let the experts speak.

> As the population ages and we see more and more professionals in our community retiring—especially the ones that have been successful and have planned for earlier retirements—that will be both an audience and a pool of resources for libraries to draw upon.
>
> —Ann Hokanson

I think that along with computer classes, medical topics will be popular. We have hosted several health screenings in our building and I was surprised at the large numbers who turned out for them (and in these cases, the health agencies came to us). Other programs that had good turnouts were on reflexology, yoga, "stress busters," and a presentation by our regional library's consultant for the blind and physically handicapped on services and materials that are available. As the population ages, these topics will become more popular. Investing is another area that has seen increased interest.

—Carol Ann Robb

The Sanibel Public Library has had great success with an adult program we call "First Friday—Stories for Grownups." A volunteer storytelling couple coordinates the program and schedules other tellers from all over the state as well as from the local area. We have often had standing-room-only audiences. As far as I know this is the only public library storytelling program geared strictly toward adults. . . . For the future at our library, I see more computer-related classes being offered as well as old-fashioned handcrafts being taught. Of course author talks and book signings are always popular.

—Pat Allen
Sanibel (Fla.) Public Library

If I had gobs of money and could hold any program I wanted, I would have English and citizenship classes for new immigrants, computer classes on specific programs, adult storytelling, a book group or two to meet different interests, parenting workshops with speakers on the importance of literacy and reading to children, and many others.

—Hillary Theyer

Personally I see some of the bread-and-butter library programming hanging around like storytimes, author visits/book signings, and book discussion groups; however, I see a more pronounced role evolving in which the public library offers more educational programming on a plethora of topics. Computer instruction

and information literacy will be a major component of future library programming.

—Michael Lambert
Foster City (Calif.) Library

Formats of the Future

Some formats will continue to be popular because they bring people together, such as book discussions and author visits. In the preceding section, we saw formats that have been traditionally associated with one audience, such as storytimes, catching on with the adults. As libraries become more and more recognizable as places that offer instruction, we may begin to expand our discussion groups into study groups.

> Library programs of the future will include more interactions with authors. I advocate creating a literary society (an example might be the Heartland Society in Chicago) that is funded by members. The literary society hosts well-known authors several times a year. I think that book clubs will evolve into book study groups in which the members choose the books they want to study in depth over time.
>
> —Cecilia Wiltzius

Delivery Methods of the Future

Our patrons have become very diverse in the ways in which they prefer to use their libraries. Some of them find us essential, yet they rarely if ever set foot inside our buildings. We will need to investigate whether these patrons want their library programs delivered to their computers at home or at work. (At the same time, we will have to monitor the digital divide, remembering that some of our patrons turn to us for technology that they do not have at home.) In what ways will technology affect and enhance programming?

> We will soon make Chapter-a-Day available to our patrons. It's an online book club for adult popular fiction and nonfiction. Their Web site is www.chapteraday.com. We hope to have it in place soon on our Web site: tblc.org/opl.
>
> —Janet Bergeron

Emulating the *New York Times* books site, quality adult programming will be held on the Web. Live book and author chats, discussion clubs, author appearances, poetry circles, and readers advisory interactions are examples of adult programs that work well on the Web.

—Cecilia Wiltzius

Other libraries are working in mediums other than the Internet. Perhaps your patrons would like to have their book discussion held live on their local cable television station. Preferably, the studio would take calls from the viewing audience, so that they can participate in the discussion as well. I participated in such an endeavor a few years back. It was a collaborative effort between the New York Public Library and a Staten Island cable station. Other libraries are also experimenting with television. Cloquet (Minn.) Public Library taped a program for the local cable access station, and it has since been shown several times.

Futuristic Funding

Creative marketing is the combination to the safe that holds our funding. Money will come our way, if we learn how to best make our case for funding. We can probably work even harder educating our administrators, library foundations, and other funding sources about our programs and the benefits they bring into our communities.

It will be important for programs to have institutional support in order to thrive. That support must be financial, either through tax dollars, in-kind donations, or fund-raising and grants.

—Cecilia Wiltzius

We can put together annual reports and presentations that show the ongoing success of our programs. We can demonstrate that programming is a popular and cost-effective service. Sponsors know that libraries and library services, such as programming, are popular with the community. Libraries can help sponsors generate money. A foundation, for example, that supports libraries can use this support as a fund-raising tool when they seek their own donations. People give to organizations that give to libraries.

Good luck with planning your programming future. Part 2 of this book tosses a few ideas your way. These programs are road tested. From your peers to you.

Endnote

1. University of California Regents, *PUBLIB and PUBLIB-NET Electronic Discussions: General Information* (Berkeley, Calif.: SunSITE, 1997), http://sunsite.berkeley.edu/PubLib/.

PART 2

A Collection of Five-Star Programs

YOUR PEERS HAVE GIVEN THE FOLLOWING PROGRAMS their seal of approval. When I asked for examples of excellent library programs for adults, these were the responses. Think of these programs as recipes: modify them to your patrons' tastes, alter the portions to fit your budget or your level of staffing, and then serve them up to your patrons. Bon appétit!

National Connections
Vermont Council on the Humanities

This NEH program, coordinated by the Vermont Council on the Humanities in collaboration with the American Library Association, took place in forty public libraries in twenty-six states in 1999.

DESCRIPTION OF PROGRAM

Collaboration of library, literacy provider, humanities council for adult new readers using children's books to discuss humanities themes. Led by a scholar.

TARGET AUDIENCE

Adult new readers

COST

Grant paid to bring teams from each library to training in this approach, paid for scholars, assisted with publicity.

NUMBER OF STAFF PERSONS NEEDED TO

Plan the Program:

Promote the Program:

Produce the Program (set up the room, introduce the speaker, distribute and collect evaluations, create displays in meeting room, etc.):

Varied from library to library, but typically three—literacy provider, library representative, scholar, and, in some cases, humanities council representative.

HOURS SPENT

Planning: Promoting: Producing:

We have only national data, not broken down by library, but about thirty hours per program.

PUBLICITY METHODS

Radio, cable, bookmarks, promotion at literacy centers, Web, posters, newspapers

ACCOMPANYING LIBRARY RESOURCES
(types of books, videos, etc., used to create displays)

Participants were provided with personal copies of all books read; some libraries added book bags and other reading items.

REFRESHMENTS SERVED?

Usually

AVERAGE ATTENDANCE

15

AUDIENCE EVALUATIONS/REACTIONS TO PROGRAM

New readers were inspired to use the library (these were "new" readers); they felt empowered by literature. Having read all the evaluations we were amazed at the uniform excited response to the new world of reading.

"Haunted Kansas"
Pittsburg (Kans.) Public Library

DESCRIPTION OF PROGRAM

Lisa Heitz, author of *Haunted Kansas,* spoke about her research for the book and then talked about different haunted sites across the state. After her talk, she sold and autographed copies of her book.

TARGET AUDIENCE

Adult (although the ages ranged from twelve to the late eighties)

COST

$100 (paid for by the Friends of the Library)

NUMBER OF STAFF PERSONS NEEDED TO

Plan the Program: 1

Promote the Program: 2

Produce the Program (set up the room, introduce the speaker, distribute and collect evaluations, create displays in meeting room, etc.): 3

HOURS SPENT

Planning: 3   Promoting: 3   Producing: 5

PUBLICITY METHODS

Newspaper articles, radio promos, in-house display, and flyers (both in the library and around the community)

ACCOMPANYING LIBRARY RESOURCES
(types of books, videos, etc., used to create displays)

Books dealing with the occult, ghosts, hauntings, etc.

EQUIPMENT NEEDED

Lectern with microphone, table for book signing

REFRESHMENTS SERVED?

Yes

AVERAGE ATTENDANCE

60

AUDIENCE EVALUATIONS/REACTIONS TO PROGRAM

Very positive. The story that appeared in the newspaper the following day was picked up by the AP and we received many phone calls from across the state about the program and book.

Kansas Raw, Rough, and True: A Gallery of Notorious Kansans
Pittsburg (Kans.) Public Library

DESCRIPTION OF PROGRAM

Local author Max McCoy regaled the audience with true stories of infamous Kansans, such as John Brown, William Quantrill, the Dalton Gang, the "Bloody Benders," and Hickock and Smith of *In Cold Blood* fame.

TARGET AUDIENCE

Adult (audience included upper-middle schoolers as well as high school students)

COST

$10–$15 (for supplies for displays)

NUMBER OF STAFF PERSONS NEEDED TO

Plan the Program: 2

Promote the Program: 3

Produce the Program (set up the room, introduce the speaker, distribute and collect evaluations, create displays in meeting room, etc.): 3

HOURS SPENT

Planning: 2   Promoting: 10   Producing: 6

PUBLICITY METHODS

Newspaper articles, in-house display and flyers, radio promos

ACCOMPANYING LIBRARY RESOURCES
(types of books, videos, etc., used to create displays)

Staff member made a "rogues gallery" of those persons discussed that was displayed before and during the program. Also had displays of books on Kansas history and biographies of the "notorious Kansans."

EQUIPMENT NEEDED

Lectern with microphone, easel to display pictures

REFRESHMENTS SERVED?

Yes

AVERAGE ATTENDANCE

65

AUDIENCE EVALUATIONS/REACTIONS TO PROGRAM

Extremely positive, but the speaker is well known and popular in town. The newspaper gave the program front-page coverage the next day, which generated more interest, and Max was asked to give the program to other groups as well. During the course of the program, he mentioned that he was thinking of turning his research into a book, and for months afterward, people came in asking if he had finished it yet and when could they check it out.

When the Drummers Were Women

Appleton (Wis.) Public Library

DESCRIPTION OF PROGRAM

A book/video discussion based on *When the Drummers Were Women: A Spiritual History of Rhythm* by Layne Redmond

Program 1: Dr. Jeffrey Dippmann, University of Wisconsin-Stout, Social Science Department, put the book in historical context with a discussion of the concepts of religion, myth, symbols, and rituals.

Program 2: Camille Banks, Appleton Public Library, guided the participants through the important issues of the topic.

Program 3: Camille Banks, Appleton Public Library, led a discussion of two videos: *The Fantastic World of Frame Drums* and *A Sense of Time.*

The programs were followed by a two-part workshop called "A Circle of Drums" in which participants learned to drum.

TARGET AUDIENCE

Individuals interested in religion, myth, and rituals; individuals who wanted a drumming experience

COST

Dr. Jeffrey Dippmann: $400; videos: $75; multiple copies of *When the Drummers Were Women*: $200; Circle of Drums workshop: $500.

NUMBER OF STAFF PERSONS NEEDED TO

Plan the Program: 2

Promote the Program: 2

Produce the Program (set up the room, introduce the speaker, distribute and collect evaluations, create displays in meeting room, etc.): 2

HOURS SPENT

Planning: 5   Promoting: 7   Producing: 12

PUBLICITY METHODS

Cable television public service announcement; newspaper ad; flyer; press release to newspapers; marketing letter sent to potential participants; listed in newspaper and magazine calendar of events

ACCOMPANYING LIBRARY RESOURCES
(types of books, videos, etc., used to create displays)

Books about the history of religion, mythology, rhythm, and drumming

EQUIPMENT NEEDED

TV/VCR; blackboard; overhead projector

REFRESHMENTS SERVED?

Hot beverages

AVERAGE ATTENDANCE

20

AUDIENCE EVALUATIONS/REACTIONS TO PROGRAM

Discussion leaders were rated "excellent"; "not one dull moment." Participants felt that they learned a lot from each other and wanted to continue meeting as a "story circle of women."

The Mind
Appleton (Wis.) Public Library

DESCRIPTION OF PROGRAM

A video/discussion series based on the nine-part PBS series *The Mind.* After each film, a health-care professional answered questions.

TARGET AUDIENCE

General public

COST

$525 for *The Mind*

NUMBER OF STAFF PERSONS NEEDED TO

Plan the Program: 2

Promote the Program: 3

Produce the Program (set up the room, introduce the speaker, distribute and collect evaluations, create displays in meeting room, etc.): 1

HOURS SPENT

Planning: 5   Promoting: 7   Producing: 20

PUBLICITY METHODS

Bookmarks; posters; newspaper press releases and ads; letter openers

ACCOMPANYING LIBRARY RESOURCES
(types of books, videos, etc., used to create displays)

Health topics

EQUIPMENT NEEDED

Video projector/screen

REFRESHMENTS SERVED?

Hot beverages

AVERAGE ATTENDANCE

50

AUDIENCE EVALUATIONS/REACTIONS TO PROGRAM

Uniformly positive. Participants appreciated having the health-care professional provide current information.

Adult/Young Adult Summer Reading Program
Round Rock (Tex.) Public Library System

DESCRIPTION OF PROGRAM

To encourage family literacy, we sponsor an adult summer reading program along with our children's reading program. Adults can count time reading newspapers, magazines, books (as long as it is nonwork time), as well as time spent reading to children. For every five hours spent reading, adults receive entries for various prizes given away during the summer. The prizes are solicited from local businesses and include such items as dinners for two, movie passes, or free food coupons.

TARGET AUDIENCE

Ages 17 and up

COST

Cost of reading logs

NUMBER OF STAFF PERSONS NEEDED TO

Plan the Program: 1

Promote the Program: 1

HOURS SPENT

Planning: 3   Promoting: 2   Producing: 2

PUBLICITY METHODS

Regular monthly calendars and in-house flyers; flyers were sent to the schools

REFRESHMENTS SERVED?

No

AVERAGE ATTENDANCE

We registered over 500 adults and had 224 read at least five hours during the eight-week program.

AUDIENCE EVALUATIONS/REACTIONS TO PROGRAM

We have had positive responses from adult participants. It helps parents encourage and model reading to their children. We get numerous calls about when our prize drawings will be held.

First Friday—Stories for Grownups
Sanibel (Fla.) Public Library

DESCRIPTION OF PROGRAM

The two volunteer storyteller/hosts contact one or two members of the Storytellers Guild of Florida who come and tell stories. The hosts provide about ten to fifteen minutes at the end of the program to let people in the audience tell a story if they wish.

TARGET AUDIENCE

Adults, although a few times a youngster has accompanied a parent or grandparent

COST

We pay the storyteller a $50 honorarium.

NUMBER OF STAFF PERSONS NEEDED TO

Plan the Program: None

Promote the Program: One staff person designs the PR pieces; the volunteers write the press release.

HOURS SPENT

Planning: None   Promoting: 3   Producing: None

PUBLICITY METHODS

Bookmarks, flyers, poster, newspaper articles

ACCOMPANYING LIBRARY RESOURCES
(types of books, videos, etc., used to create displays)

None

EQUIPMENT NEEDED

None

REFRESHMENTS SERVED?

Sometimes, if holiday or some special theme is used

AVERAGE ATTENDANCE

35–40

AUDIENCE EVALUATIONS/REACTIONS TO PROGRAM

Excellent; has encouraged others to be storytellers.

Adult Summer Reading Club
The Ferguson Library (Stamford, Conn.)

DESCRIPTION OF PROGRAM

A summer reading program geared to adults and established as a complement to the children's program that has been running for years. The program runs from mid-June through the end of August. Each program has its own theme, incentives, and programming. Adults are asked to read five books over the course of the summer. They come into the main library or our three branches plus the bookmobile, and register to become members of the club on specially designed registration cards. These cards are printed on both sides. One side has the person's name and address, and the other has a line for each book read. After the first, third, and final books are completed, each participant receives a small prize, such as a bookmark, pen, or notebook. These prizes change each year. The final prize is either a bookmark, mug, or other token plus an invitation to our end-of-summer celebration. All members who read the five books receive this invitation. The end-of-year celebration includes an evening of desserts or ice cream and a performance. The first few years of our program, the performance was a storyteller. But last year and this year we contracted with a performance artist. Last year we had an actress who portrayed Agatha Christie. This year we are having a magician-comedian who does a performance geared for adults. We have a kickoff event each year that features authors who discuss the craft of writing and publishing. This year, three authors who published self-help books participated. The theme was Achieving Your Personal Best.

We also run two book discussion series, one in July and one in August. These usually meet at one of the branch locations.

The main library also does a noontime book-sharing program in June that focuses on recommendations for summer reading. This program is the only daytime program. The other programs take place at 7:00 P.M.

TARGET AUDIENCE

Adults

COST

$3,000 (we are well funded by our Friends group). Cost covers refreshments, extra copies of books for the discussion, performance fees, and the big expense—incentives. The program can be adjusted to fit different budgets.

NUMBER OF STAFF PERSONS NEEDED TO

Plan the Program: Committee of 5–7 members

Promote the Program: About the same

Produce the Program (set up the room, introduce the speaker, distribute and collect evaluations, create displays in meeting room, etc.): Our program is run by the Adult and Reader Services department, which has five full-time members plus four part-time people. The branches take care of their programs. Usually from one to two staff members are needed for the evening programs.

HOURS SPENT

Planning: Promoting: Producing:

We begin planning in January so that the program can be in place by mid-June. We have never kept track of the exact amount of time needed. However, to do a good program you need time and more than one person to produce the program. Time is also needed to select a theme and design flyers and other printed pieces.

PUBLICITY METHODS

We do one complete flyer with all dates and events listed. The program is also promoted through our newsletter, published every two months. The children's room does extensive promotion through the schools and encourages the children to tell their parents about the Adult Club. We post big signs and talk up the program at our public service desks. We also hand-deliver packets of flyers to the bookstores and our local mall. Information is posted on our Web site, where patrons can register and list their book titles. Our PR department creates large posters that are scattered throughout the library.

ACCOMPANYING LIBRARY RESOURCES
(types of books, videos, etc., used to create displays)

We display all kinds of books and talking books on our summer reading display. We have book bins of past favorite titles as well as staff recommendations. We also create author-list bookmarks for handouts as well as other types of bibliographies.

EQUIPMENT NEEDED

Tables; bulletin boards are helpful as are bookmark holders. We also cover tables with tablecloths. Our theme this year was "Carry the Torch—Read!" to go with the Olympic Games.

We used the stars and stripes theme to decorate the area where we set up our display. We also used pictures from our picture file to decorate the walls with Olympic athletes and symbols.

REFRESHMENTS SERVED?

Yes

AVERAGE ATTENDANCE

Our kickoff event usually averages from 60 to 75 participants. Book discussions attract 15–26 people. Our end-of-year event totaled between 100 and 125. Usually we have about 350 people who sign up and participate in the program. Not all members come to the programs.

AUDIENCE EVALUATIONS/REACTIONS TO PROGRAM

Reactions have been very positive, and we have a lot of repeat participants each year. We did surveys and evaluations the first several years of the program and tried to tailor the program to suggestions from our patrons.

Introduction to Feng Shui
Jefferson Parish Library (Metairie, La.)

DESCRIPTION OF PROGRAM

A practitioner of the art of Feng Shui did a slide presentation on what Feng Shui is and gave the basics of how to apply it to home or office design.

TARGET AUDIENCE

Homeowners and businesspeople

COST

None

NUMBER OF STAFF PERSONS NEEDED TO

Plan the Program: One staff member coordinated the program: invited speaker, booked meeting room, sent letter of confirmation to the speaker, and sent thank you to the speaker after the program.

Promote the Program: One staff member (coordinator) sent PSAs to the electronic media and newspapers; created flyers and posters (17 by 22 inches).

Produce the Program (set up the room, introduce the speaker, distribute and collect evaluations, create displays in meeting room, etc.): One maintenance person set up the chairs and podium. Coordinator introduced the speaker.

HOURS SPENT

Planning: 3   Promoting: 4

Producing: 5 (two locations)

PUBLICITY METHODS

Press releases and PSAs sent to newspapers, television, radio; flyers, posters, and bibliography created

ACCOMPANYING LIBRARY RESOURCES
(types of books, videos, etc., used to create displays)

Table display of books on the topic

EQUIPMENT NEEDED

Speaker needed to provide slide projector and slides; screens provided at our two locations

REFRESHMENTS SERVED?

No

AVERAGE ATTENDANCE

110

AUDIENCE EVALUATIONS/REACTIONS TO PROGRAM

Audience response was positive, with many questions for the presenter. The presenter discouraged individual detailed questions in favor of contacting the participants after the program.

Louisiana Mounds: A 5,000-Year-Old Tradition
Jefferson Parish Library (Metairie, La.)

DESCRIPTION OF PROGRAM

Slide presentation about ancient man-made mounds located throughout Louisiana. Part of 1999 Louisiana Archaeology Week, sponsored by State Division of Archaeology.

TARGET AUDIENCE

Adults

COST

None

NUMBER OF STAFF PERSONS NEEDED TO

Plan the Program: One staff member coordinated the program by booking the meeting room. State Division of Archaeology invited speakers, confirmed bookings, arranged titles, etc.

Promote the Program: Coordinator sent press releases and PSAs to newspapers and electronic media. State Division of Archaeology created posters and programs. Community Relations Department wrote an article for library newsletter.

Produce the Program (set up the room, introduce the speaker, distribute and collect evaluations, create displays in meeting room, etc.): One maintenance person set up the room. Coordinator introduced speaker and handled evaluations.

HOURS SPENT

Planning: 4   Promoting: 4   Producing: 2

PUBLICITY METHODS

Program book and posters were created and distributed by the State Division of Archaeology; press releases and PSAs were sent to newspapers, television, radio; letters were sent to schools; program was listed on the library Web page calendar of events; program was listed on a local-interest Internet site

ACCOMPANYING LIBRARY RESOURCES
(types of books, videos, etc., used to create displays)

None

EQUIPMENT NEEDED

Speaker provided slide projector and slides; library provided screen and podium with microphone.

REFRESHMENTS SERVED?

No

AVERAGE ATTENDANCE

63

AUDIENCE EVALUATIONS/REACTIONS TO PROGRAM

Audience enjoyed the speaker and the topic.

Historical Spotlight with Buddy Stall/Ed Clancy
Jefferson Parish Library (Metairie, La.)

DESCRIPTION OF PROGRAM

Last-minute substitution of speaker. Speaker gave an anecdotal history of Jefferson Parish and the New Orleans metropolitan area. Part of the celebration of the Jefferson Parish Library's fiftieth anniversary.

TARGET AUDIENCE

Adults and teens from Jefferson Parish

COST

None (as long as there were at least fifty participants in the audience)

NUMBER OF STAFF PERSONS NEEDED TO

Plan the Program: One staff member coordinated contacting the speaker, booking the meeting room, sending the confirmation to the speaker, and sending the thank you to the speaker after the program. Library Director had to sign a release.

Promote the Program: Coordinator sent press releases and PSAs to newspapers and electronic media and letters to schools. Community Services wrote an article for the library newsletter.

Produce the Program (set up the room, introduce the speaker, distribute and collect evaluations, create displays in meeting room, etc.): One maintenance staff person set up the room. Coordinator introduced the speaker and handled evaluations.

HOURS SPENT

Planning: 5   Promoting: 4   Producing: 2

PUBLICITY METHODS

Press releases and PSAs sent to newspapers, television, radio; flyers, posters, and bibliography created; article in library newsletter; letters to schools; calendar entry on library Web page; calendar entry on local-interest Web site

ACCOMPANYING LIBRARY RESOURCES
(types of books, videos, etc., used to create displays)
None

EQUIPMENT NEEDED

Podium and microphone provided at our location.

REFRESHMENTS SERVED?

No

AVERAGE ATTENDANCE

53

AUDIENCE EVALUATIONS/REACTIONS TO PROGRAM

Even with the change in speaker, the audience laughed and enjoyed the talk, and asked when the next speaker would appear at the library. Began a library mailing list.

What Used to Be Here? Historic Sites of Jefferson Parish Libraries
Jefferson Parish Library (Metairie, La.)

DESCRIPTION OF PROGRAM

A historical archaeologist presented slides of maps of lands upon which today's library branches were built. Part of the celebration of the library's fiftieth anniversary.

TARGET AUDIENCE

Adults and teens

COST

$75 per hour at each location

NUMBER OF STAFF PERSONS NEEDED TO

Plan the Program: One staff member coordinated contacting the speaker, booking the meeting room, sending the confirmation to the speaker, and sending the thank you to the speaker after the program. Second staff member had to arrange for payment of the speaker.

Promote the Program: Coordinator sent press releases and PSAs to newspapers and electronic media and letters to schools. Community Services wrote an article for the library newsletter.

Produce the Program (set up the room, introduce the speaker, distribute and collect evaluations, create displays in meeting room, etc.): One maintenance staff person set up the room. Coordinator introduced the speaker and handled evaluations.

HOURS SPENT

Planning: 4   Promoting: 5

Producing: 5 (2 programs)

PUBLICITY METHODS

Press releases and PSAs sent to newspapers, television, radio; flyers, posters, and bibliography created; article in library newsletter; letters to schools; calendar entry on library Web page; calendar entry on local-interest Web site

ACCOMPANYING LIBRARY RESOURCES
(types of books, videos, etc., used to create displays)

Display of books written by the speaker

EQUIPMENT NEEDED

Library provided slide projector, screen, and podium with microphone.

REFRESHMENTS SERVED?

No

AVERAGE ATTENDANCE

95

AUDIENCE EVALUATIONS/REACTIONS TO PROGRAM

Audience enjoyed the speaker and wanted more historical programs.

N'Awlins' Own: Meet Frank Davis

Jefferson Parish Library (Metairie, La.)

DESCRIPTION OF PROGRAM

The author of five cookbooks, a celebrated fisherman and local television program host, spoke of his work and varied professions.

TARGET AUDIENCE

Adults

COST

None (usually $2,500 to conventions)

NUMBER OF STAFF PERSONS NEEDED TO

Plan the Program: One staff member coordinated contacting the speaker, booking the meeting room, sending the confirmation to the speaker, and sending the thank you to the speaker after the program.

Promote the Program: Coordinator sent press releases and PSAs to newspapers and electronic media; wrote article for Friends' newsletter. Community Services wrote an article for the library newsletter.

Produce the Program (set up the room, introduce the speaker, distribute and collect evaluations, create displays in meeting room, etc.): One maintenance staff person set up the room. Coordinator introduced the speaker and handled evaluations.

HOURS SPENT

Planning: 6   Promoting: 4   Producing: 2

PUBLICITY METHODS

Press releases and PSAs sent to newspapers, television, radio; flyers, posters, and bibliography created; article in library newsletter; calendar entry on library Web page; calendar entry on local-interest Web site

ACCOMPANYING LIBRARY RESOURCES
(types of books, videos, etc., used to create displays)

Display of books written by the speaker

EQUIPMENT NEEDED

Library provided a podium with microphone.

REFRESHMENTS SERVED?

No

AVERAGE ATTENDANCE

140

AUDIENCE EVALUATIONS/REACTIONS TO PROGRAM

Audience enjoyed the program and the speaker; asked for more speakers at future programs.

Antiques and Collectibles Appraisal Fair
Rocky River (Ohio) Public Library

DESCRIPTION OF PROGRAM

Our "Antiques and Collectibles Appraisal Fair" invited people to bring their treasures to our auditorium from 1:00 P.M. to 3:00 P.M. on a Saturday afternoon. We hired five appraisers, each of whom had expertise with such items as china, silver, and art.

As people came through the doors, we matched them up, by item, to the most appropriate appraiser and gave each person a number. We color-coded the numbered slips of paper with each individual appraiser's sign so people knew exactly where to go when we announced, for instance, "Blue 5 through 10 can join the line." We called them up in groups to keep the line moving. Even though people were allowed to bring two items, they met with only one appraiser because of time constraints. But because each appraiser had a minimum of thirty years in the business, even if that second item wasn't in his or her area of expertise, the appraiser was almost always able to impart some information.

As numbers were called, people approached their appraiser seated at a table and had their items appraised.

TARGET AUDIENCE

Adults

COST

$100 per appraiser

NUMBER OF STAFF PERSONS NEEDED TO

Plan the Program: 1

Promote the Program: 1

Produce the Program (set up the room, introduce the speaker, distribute and collect evaluations, create displays in meeting room, etc.): 2 to distribute and call the numbers; 2 to set up the room

HOURS SPENT

Planning: 8   Promoting: 2   Producing: 5

PUBLICITY METHODS

Signage and flyers throughout the library; press releases to local newspapers; flyers to area antique shops

ACCOMPANYING LIBRARY RESOURCES
(types of books, videos, etc., used to create displays)

Books on antiques were displayed on units throughout the library.

EQUIPMENT NEEDED

One 8-by-12-foot table per appraiser

REFRESHMENTS SERVED?

No

AVERAGE ATTENDANCE

300 patrons attended our first fair; 200 came to our second.

AUDIENCE EVALUATIONS/REACTIONS
TO PROGRAM

People commented on how much they appreciated this opportunity and were pleased that they weren't charged for it. Many simply were thankful to learn more about their possessions from the knowledgeable appraisers we found at area antique shops.

Music at the Library
San Marcos (Tex.) Public Library

DESCRIPTION OF PROGRAM

Once each month, from September through May, we have a local musician play for an hour. We select a variety of musicians representing various musical styles, ages, and backgrounds.

TARGET AUDIENCE

Families, music lovers, general library patrons

COST

About $6 (for refreshments)

NUMBER OF STAFF PERSONS NEEDED TO

Plan the Program: One staff member coordinated the program.

Promote the Program: One staff member promoted the program by an announcement in the monthly newsletter, flyers in the library, PSAs sent to local newspapers, radio, and cable TV, and bank marquee signs.

Produce the Program (set up the room, introduce the speaker, distribute and collect evaluations, create displays in meeting room, etc.): Two library clerks set up the room with chairs; the program coordinator sets up the refreshments and introduces the musicians.

HOURS SPENT

Planning: 2   Promoting: 3   Producing: 2

PUBLICITY METHODS

Library newsletter and flyers in library. An article (with photo, if available) is submitted to the local newspaper, community calendar entries in other area papers and the local cable station, and a short advertisement on two local bank marquee signs. Sometimes we will actually get flyers to the local music store as well!

ACCOMPANYING LIBRARY RESOURCES
(types of books, videos, etc., used to create displays)
None

EQUIPMENT NEEDED

The musicians are responsible for bringing their own sound equipment if they want it.

REFRESHMENTS SERVED?

Yes—cookies and lemonade

AVERAGE ATTENDANCE

40 to 60, children included

AUDIENCE EVALUATIONS/REACTIONS TO PROGRAM

We have many local residents who make it a point to attend this program each month. We want to provide an alternative setting for local music so that people who do not want to go to bars or who have families and cannot stay out late can enjoy the current local music the community has to offer.

Creative Writing Workshops
San Marcos (Tex.) Public Library

DESCRIPTION OF PROGRAM

Weekly workshop, open to the public on a sign-up basis to limit classes to about fifteen participants. A faculty member or graduate student from the local university volunteers about once a year to offer a writing workshop to the public at the library.

TARGET AUDIENCE

General public

COST

None

NUMBER OF STAFF PERSONS NEEDED TO

Plan the Program: One staff member coordinated the program.

Promote the Program: The Patron Services librarian creates the monthly newsletter, flyers, and public service announcements to go to local newspapers, radio, and cable TV.

Produce the Program (set up the room, introduce the speaker, distribute and collect evaluations, create displays in meeting room, etc.): One—the classes usually meet in the conference room where there is a large table with chairs and a dry-erase board. Workshop presenters introduce themselves. If there are any copies to make, the Public Services librarian arranges for those to be made.

HOURS SPENT

Planning: 3   Promoting: 2   Producing: 2

PUBLICITY METHODS

Monthly library newsletter, in-house flyers, newspaper article, community calendar entries in area papers, radio, and cable TV

ACCOMPANYING LIBRARY RESOURCES

(types of books, videos, etc., used to create displays)

None

EQUIPMENT NEEDED

None

REFRESHMENTS SERVED?

No

AVERAGE ATTENDANCE

12 to 15 on a weekly basis for several weeks (usually six to eight weeks)

AUDIENCE EVALUATIONS/REACTIONS TO PROGRAM

These programs are very popular and we have to turn away people each time we offer them.

Yoga
San Marcos (Tex.) Public Library

DESCRIPTION OF PROGRAM

We have a volunteer who offers free yoga classes two Fridays a month. She is a certified yoga instructor and acupuncturist.

TARGET AUDIENCE

General public

COST

None

NUMBER OF STAFF PERSONS NEEDED TO

Plan the Program: One staff member coordinated the program with the volunteer.

Promote the Program: The Patron Services librarian creates the monthly newsletter and in-house flyers.

Produce the Program (set up the room, introduce the speaker, distribute and collect evaluations, create displays in meeting room, etc.): None

HOURS SPENT

Planning: 30 minutes   Promoting: 30 minutes

Producing: 1.5 hours every other week

PUBLICITY METHODS

Monthly library newsletter, in-house flyers

ACCOMPANYING LIBRARY RESOURCES
(types of books, videos, etc., used to create displays)

None

EQUIPMENT NEEDED

None

REFRESHMENTS SERVED?

No

AVERAGE ATTENDANCE

12

AUDIENCE EVALUATIONS/REACTIONS
TO PROGRAM

We have an ongoing appreciation for this class. At first we just offered it for a few months, but so many people were disappointed when it ended that the instructor agreed to continue the class. She has been offering it for three years and regularly takes a vacation from it for only one month during the year. She also gives the class next door at our community activity center on a fee basis.

Paper Card Crafting
San Marcos (Tex.) Public Library

DESCRIPTION OF PROGRAM

We have a volunteer who offers paper card and ornament crafting once or twice a year.

TARGET AUDIENCE

General public, mostly women

COST

$5. We buy card stock for the craft and copy the patterns needed for each participant over at city hall. The volunteer brings her own stamping supplies.

NUMBER OF STAFF PERSONS NEEDED TO

Plan the Program: One staff member coordinated the program with the volunteer.

Promote the Program: The Patron Services librarian creates the monthly newsletter, in-house flyers, PSAs for local newspapers, radio, and cable TV.

Produce the Program (set up the room, introduce the speaker, distribute and collect evaluations, create displays in meeting room, etc.): The Patron Services librarian instructs two library clerks on how to set up chairs and tables for an adult craft event, and has the handouts and paper ready for the class.

HOURS SPENT

Planning: 2   Promoting: 1   Producing: 2

PUBLICITY METHODS

Monthly library newsletter, in-house flyers, PSA in local papers, radio, and cable TV

ACCOMPANYING LIBRARY RESOURCES
(types of books, videos, etc., used to create displays)

Sometimes we will display a variety of books on paper crafts and stamping.

EQUIPMENT NEEDED

Paper cutter, scissors, pencils, patterns, rulers, glue sticks, rubber stamps, stamp pads, card stock, and examples of the finished craft

REFRESHMENTS SERVED?

No

AVERAGE ATTENDANCE

15 to 20

AUDIENCE EVALUATIONS/REACTIONS TO PROGRAM

Each time she offers the class we have a full room. She is a very talented artist with paper and stamping techniques and brings her own stamping equipment. Everyone really enjoys what she has to offer. (She also decorates our Christmas tree each year with her own original paper ornaments created especially for us.)

Journal Writing and Memoirs
San Marcos (Tex.) Public Library

DESCRIPTION OF PROGRAM

Singular workshop, open to the public on a sign-up basis to limit classes to about fifteen participants. We have a local writer who occasionally offers to present a onetime workshop on writing journals or memoirs. She is a professional writer and has columns in a variety of newspapers and magazines.

TARGET AUDIENCE

General public

COST

None

NUMBER OF STAFF PERSONS NEEDED TO

Plan the Program: One staff member coordinated the program.

Promote the Program: The Patron Services librarian creates the monthly newsletter, flyers, and public service announcements to go to local newspapers, radio, and cable TV.

Produce the Program (set up the room, introduce the speaker, distribute and collect evaluations, create displays in meeting room, etc.): 1—the classes usually meet in the conference room where there is a large table with chairs and a dry-erase board. Workshop presenters introduce themselves. If there are any handouts, the Public Services librarian arranges for those to be made.

HOURS SPENT

Planning: 3   Promoting: 2   Producing: 4

PUBLICITY METHODS

Monthly library newsletter, in-house flyers, newspaper article, community calendar entries in area papers, radio, and cable TV

ACCOMPANYING LIBRARY RESOURCES
(types of books, videos, etc., used to create displays)

None

EQUIPMENT NEEDED

None

REFRESHMENTS SERVED?

No

AVERAGE ATTENDANCE

10

AUDIENCE EVALUATIONS/REACTIONS TO PROGRAM

Program participants have enjoyed the workshops and are encouraged to write about their own experiences.

Home Buying Workshops
San Marcos (Tex.) Public Library

DESCRIPTION OF PROGRAM

We had a series of workshops on the various aspects of home buying that were organized by a local title company. Each month was a different topic, such as understanding a mortgage and the mechanics involved in buying a home.

TARGET AUDIENCE

General public

COST

None

NUMBER OF STAFF PERSONS NEEDED TO

Plan the Program: One staff member coordinated the program with the title company representative who scheduled the various program presenters.

Promote the Program: The Patron Services librarian creates the monthly newsletter, flyers, and public service announcements to go to local newspapers, radio, and cable TV.

HOURS SPENT

Planning: 3   Promoting: 2   Producing: 4

PUBLICITY METHODS

Monthly library newsletter, in-house flyers, newspaper article, and community calendar entries in area newspapers, radio, and cable TV

ACCOMPANYING LIBRARY RESOURCES
(types of books, videos, etc., used to create displays)

We set up displays of library books on various home-related topics.

EQUIPMENT NEEDED

None

REFRESHMENTS SERVED?

No

AVERAGE ATTENDANCE

10

AUDIENCE EVALUATIONS/REACTIONS TO PROGRAM

Most of the attendees were pleased to be able to acquire this type of information in an informal setting. (*Note:* One of the stipulations for using our meeting room is that no one may use the room for "for-profit" purposes. Unfortunately, one of the presenters was very pushy about a business and we did not schedule anymore workshops after a patron complained.)

World War II: As Recalled by Local Heroes
Rochester (Minn.) Public Library

DESCRIPTION OF PROGRAM

A panel of three local World War II veterans spoke about their wartime experiences. They also answered questions. Glen Miller served in the South Pacific; Bill McConahey, M.D., served as a battle surgeon in Normandy; and Chris Stapleton was stationed at Pearl Harbor. The program was presented on December 7, Pearl Harbor Day.

TARGET AUDIENCE

Local citizens, veterans, high school students, and seniors

COST   None

NUMBER OF STAFF PERSONS NEEDED TO

Plan the Program: 1

Promote the Program: 2

Produce the Program (set up the room, introduce the speaker, distribute and collect evaluations, create displays in meeting room, etc.): 3

HOURS SPENT

Planning: 3   Promoting: 3   Producing: 3

PUBLICITY METHODS

PSAs were sent to local event magazines and the newspaper. Event posters were placed in the library, in the local VFW, and in local high schools.

ACCOMPANYING LIBRARY RESOURCES
(types of books, videos, etc., used to create displays)

There was an entryway display of World War II books, movies, and music for two weeks before the event. There was a window display of war memorabilia loaned by the panelists for three weeks before the event. On the evening of the program, both displays were moved to the auditorium where the event was held.

EQUIPMENT NEEDED

3 microphones

REFRESHMENTS SERVED?

No

AVERAGE ATTENDANCE

280

AUDIENCE EVALUATIONS/REACTIONS TO PROGRAM

Audience loved it. There was a diverse group of people from high school students to seniors. The program facilitated great cross-generational dialogue. The event also drew a lot of men who don't generally attend library events.

You're Ready to Roll!

There you have it. Now it's time to take one of these programs out for a test drive. Or, create your own itinerary. The journey ahead should be an exciting one. Best of luck.

RESOURCE DIRECTORY

THE FOLLOWING RESOURCES COMPLEMENT THE information that is included in this book. The directory is arranged to coincide with the chapters that you have just read. These sources were selected because they provide valuable information in a coherent manner. I have used many of these resources many times over the years. I hope they will serve you as well as they have served me.

Getting Started

Brown, Barbara J. *Programming for Librarians: A How-to-Do-It Manual.* New York: Neal-Schuman, 1992.

A good, concise guide to library programming. Also contains information on programming for children and young adults. The information provided on community analysis is particularly helpful.

McGovern, Gail, Amy Bernath, Kenna Forsyth, Laura Kimberly, and Kathleen Stacey. *Program Planning: Tips for Librarians.* Chicago: Continuing Library Education Network Exchange Round Table, American Library Association, 1997.

This publication is very brief—25 pages plus appendices. Geared primarily toward libraries that are planning an in-house staff development or training activity. Offers tips on how to conduct a needs assessment, design the program content, and set up a room (both seating and equipment). Good resource for librarians who intend to create and present the content themselves.

O'Donnell, Peggy, and Patsy Read. *Planning Library Programs.* Chicago: Public Library Association, 1979.

This title is no longer in print, but copies are available via interlibrary loan. Another slim publication (49 pages). Although the authors encourage the reader to host humanities programs sponsored by the National Endowment for the Humanities, this work offers some great nuggets of information on programming in general. Highlights include a community survey worksheet and a chart that helps the reader select the best program format.

Painter, Chris, and Maureen Crocker. *Rated "A" for Adult: A Guide to Library Programming.* Pinecliff, Colo.: Colorado Library Association, 1991.

No longer in print. A brief, 51-page manual that contains good, basic information. Includes information on how to get program ideas, what programs will work in your community, and a programming checklist. Beware: the 16-page programming resource list contains organizations that are predominantly located in Colorado.

Robotham, John S., and Lydia LaFleur. *Library Programs: How to Select, Plan, and Produce Them.* 2nd ed. Metuchen, N.J.: Scarecrow, 1981.

Although no longer in print, this book is a wonderful resource. The first part of the book is organized by program formats. This is the book's greatest strength. The authors lead you through what you need to know if you intend to host a discussion group, film series, workshop, etc. For each format, the authors discuss staffing needs, equipment needs, space requirements, suggestions for topics, etc. The second part of the book explains how to select and find programs. The third part offers advice on how to produce the program.

Rubin, Rhea Joyce. *Humanities Programming: A How-to-Do-It Manual.* New York: Neal-Schuman, 1997.

Another strong title from Neal-Schuman. Although geared toward humanities programs, this book offers good advice on planning, funding, budgeting, publicizing, and evaluating programs that can be used for any type of adult programming.

RUSA-SUPS Services to Adults Committee. *Adult Programming: A Manual for Libraries.* Chicago: Reference and User Services Association, American Library Association, 1997.

Confession: I served on the committee that wrote this manual, so I am quite fond of it. Yet another slender publication (57 pages), this manual leads you through the adult programming process from beginning to end. Contains a set of appendices with examples of a programming policy, a program planning worksheet, a program planning checklist, a press release, a PSA, and program evaluation forms.

Demographics

Public Library Association. *Statistical Report '93: Public Library Data Service.* Chicago: Public Library Association, 1993.

If your library is one of the 500-plus included in this report, then take a look. You will quickly be able to find information about program attendance, the age and educational level of your population, the percentage of the population with library cards, etc.

Tuggle, Ann Montgomery, and Dawn Hansen Heller. *Grand Schemes and Nitty-Gritty Details: Library PR That Works.* Littleton, Colo.: Libraries Unlimited, 1987.

Although no longer in print, this title is worth a look if you can locate a copy. The purpose of this book is to ensure that your library runs a successful public relations program. The book stresses the importance of making connections with your community. One section called "Fact-Finding and Research" gives some excellent tips on conducting surveys.

United States. Bureau of the Census. *County and City Data Book: A Statistical Abstract Supplement.* Washington, D.C.: U.S. Bureau of the Census, published annually.

Much of the data included come from the 1990 Census of Population and Housing. Hopefully, an update is on its way with data from the 2000 census. You can spend a week gathering data from this source—unemployment rates, percentage of the population who speak a language other than English, information on race, number of people who work from home, etc. Just browsing this source will give you programming ideas.

Budgeting and Funding

American Library Association and The Taft Group Staff. *The Big Book of Library Grant Money 2002–2003.* Detroit: Gale Group, 2001.

Includes thousands of philanthropic programs that have either given grants to libraries in recent years or list libraries as potential recipients.

Annual Register of Grant Support. New Providence, N.J.: R. R. Bowker, published annually.

This massive work contains over 3,000 grant support programs. Fortunately, "libraries" is one of the words indexed, so you can zero-in on funding sources for libraries. Also contains a section on proposal writing.

Barber, Peggy, and Linda D. Crowe. *Getting Your Grant: A How-to-Do-It Manual for Librarians.* New York: Neal-Schuman, 1993.

Although this title is getting older, the step-by-step approach, geared specifically toward libraries, is very helpful. Takes you from the idea stage, through the grant-writing process, and into the follow-through stage, which includes publicizing your newly funded project. Also includes many checklists and sample grant applications.

Dolnick, Sandy, ed. *Friends of Libraries Sourcebook.* 3rd ed. Chicago: American Library Association, 1996.

This title is written as a guide to be used by Friends organizations. It does include a chapter on programming. This chapter is useful as it gives you ideas about the types of programs that are attractive to Friends groups. Another chapter on fund-raising includes programming ideas that can raise funds, such as meet-the-author events. This book should help you identify program ideas that your Friends group will be interested in sponsoring.

Farmer, Lesley S. J. *When Your Library Budget Is Almost Zero.* Englewood, Colo.: Libraries Unlimited, 1993.

Contains a section on offering library programs. Also offers good advice on how to ask funders for money and what to do after you get your money.

The Foundation Directory. New York: Foundation Center, published annually.

Includes over 10,000 foundations. Each of the foundations listed possesses at least $2 million in assets or gives at least $200,000 a year. "Libraries" is an indexed term.

Miner, Lynn E., Jeremy T. Miner, and Jerry Griffith. *Proposal Planning and Writing.* 2nd ed. Phoenix: Oryx, 1998.

A good all-in-one source. Offers detailed information on how to write proposals. Differentiates by type of proposal: foundation versus corporate versus government. Also lists resources to use when searching for funds, including information on Internet sources.

Prentice, Ann E. *Financial Planning for Libraries.* 2nd ed. Lanham, Md.: Scarecrow, 1996.

An in-depth guide to financial planning. Provides a thorough chapter on sources of library funding (taxes, state funding, federal funding, private funding, and fee-based services).

Rounds, Richard S. *Basic Budgeting Practices for Librarians.* 2nd ed. Chicago: American Library Association, 1994.

Although geared toward an administrator who is developing the overall library budget, this is a good source that leads you step-by-step through the budgeting process. Covers community profiling, presenting your budget to the decision makers, and managing the budget.

Warner, Alice S. *Budgeting: A How-to-Do-It Manual for Librarians.* New York: Neal-Schuman, 1998.

Written for librarians, this title offers detailed assistance in establishing budgets. It also offers guidance on how to manage funding that is achieved through grants, endowments, and fundraising events.

Selecting a Topic

Chase's Calendar of Events. Chicago: Contemporary Books, published annually.

This is an amazing resource. You can really use it a couple of ways. You can browse through the months to find festivals, anniversaries, and celebrity birthdays for each month of the year. You can then plan a program around one of these events. Or, you might already have a program idea in mind, such as a cooking program on making desserts. When should you have the program? Check *Chase's*. It will tell you that October is National Dessert Month!

Your Target Audience

Alire, Camila, and Orlando Archibeque. *Serving Latino Communities: A How-to-Do-It Manual for Librarians.* New York: Neal-Schuman, 1998.

I love this book. I've read it cover to cover at least twice. A great book to read if you are just beginning to serve a Latino population. Offers demographic information on Latinos; provides in-depth information on how to conduct a needs assessment; includes programming ideas and resources; offers information on effective outreach; includes funding tips; and much, much more!

Rubin, Rhea Joyce. *Intergenerational Programming: A How-to-Do-It Manual for Librarians.* New York: Neal-Schuman, 1993.

Offers detailed information on providing intergenerational programs. Provides good information on how to partner with other agencies in your community. Provides detailed examples of successful programs from around the United States. Also provides program planning worksheets on specific types of intergenerational programs, such as family literacy projects and history programs.

Trotta, Marcia. *Managing Library Outreach Programs: A How-to-Do-It Manual for Librarians.* New York: Neal-Schuman, 1993.

Although it focuses on outreach services for children and young adults, this title is a good resource to consult if you are just getting started with outreach services. Includes a history of outreach services in libraries. Provides information on conducting a community needs assessment. Also offers insight into the importance of forging community partnerships; includes examples of actual outreach programs; and explains how to develop outreach staff.

Identifying Performers

Encyclopedia of Associations: Regional, State, and Local Organizations. Detroit, Mich.: Gale, published annually.

I use this constantly. It lists over 22,000 associations. Just about any topic—diabetes, dance, or darts—will have one to several associations dedicated to it. Many of these associations will have local chapters. Give them a call. They might be happy to supply a speaker or performer.

The Whole Person Catalog No. 4: The Librarian's Source for Information about Cultural Programming for Adults. Chicago: American Library Association, Public Programs Office, [1999].

Lists many discussion and literary programs developed by libraries, state humanities councils, historical societies, and other groups. Also includes contact information. If you find a program that looks interesting, this book will help you learn more about it. It might be funded by an agency such as the NEH or your state humanities council. They might be able to fund the program at your library and provide you with a scholar to lead the discussion series.

Publicity

Field, Selma G., and Edwin M. Field. *Publicity Manual for Libraries: A Comprehensive Professional Guide to Communications . . . a Book That No Library Should Be Without.* Monticello, N.Y.: Knowledge Network Press, 1993.

A great, step-by-step resource, this book will help you write news releases and news stories, target your story to radio, and evaluate the success of your publicity efforts. Includes many sample press releases.

Leerburger, Benedict A. *Promoting and Marketing the Library.* Rev. ed. Boston: G. K. Hall, 1989.

Contains good information on publicity techniques. Also contains a 36-page chapter called "Special Programs and Events."

Walters, Suzanne. *Marketing: A How-to-Do-It Manual for Librarians.* New York: Neal-Schuman, 1992.

This manual leads you through the marketing process, which involves talking to our customers and developing services that meet their needs. It also involves strategies (public relations, advertising, direct mailings, etc.) that your library can use to ensure that patrons are aware of the services you offer. Sample marketing plans are included.

Examples of Successful Adult Programs

Public Library Association, Small and Medium-Sized Libraries, 1986 Conference Program Committee. *Adults Only: Program Ideas of Interest to Your Adult Patrons.* Chicago: Public Library Association, 1986.

Out of print. Contains ten detailed examples of programs for adults, including descriptions of the programs, equipment and staff needed, publicity used, etc. Two of the examples are a "Chef of the Month" program and a series of programs on antiques. Also includes guidelines to consider when planning programs, a program planning worksheet, and staff and patron evaluation forms.

INDEX